THE UNIQUENESS OF WOMAN

To Anne
Jesus loves you

OTHER BOOKS BY
JENNIFER ABIGAIL LAWSON-WALLACE

Free To Serve: God's Liberated Woman

Designed For Purpose

Sons Of God, Our Ultimate Identity As Women In Christ

Women Who Met Jesus

Contact us by email to find out more about purchasing any of them: info@womenintune.org

THE UNIQUENESS OF WOMAN

JENNIFER ABIGAIL LAWSON-WALLACE

WWW.WOMENINTUNE.ORG

The Uniqueness Of Woman

Published by
NOBRICH
CEDARS HOUSE PUBLISHING
149 Canterbury Road
London, E10 5AH
info@womenintune.org

Bible Versions Used in this book include:
NKJV - New King James Version,
NASB - New American Standard Bible
AMP - Amplified Bible
NLT - New Living Translation
TPT - The Passion Translation
The Voice

All Hebrew definitions are taken from *Strong's Exhaustive Concordance of the Bible.*

ISBN: 978-0-9558369-5-4

Cover design by *Nobelle Wallace Graphics*
Printed in the United Kingdom

CONTENTS

DEDICATION

To Jackie Arnot and everyone who encouraged me to write this book.

ACKNOWLEDGMENTS

Thank You, to God, our Father, for trusting me with this task of restoring, raising and releasing women to serve Him. He always empowers me to fulfil His will, as I endeavour to serve Him; without His leading and grace, this book would never have been written.

Thank you to my husband Rev Cobby E Wallace and family, who always stand with me, in everything. Thank you to my beloved daughter, Nobelle for helping prepare the manuscript. Thanks to Rev Darlene Erbynn for the advice and counsel given. Thanks to my friends, Jen Gaskin and Glenys London for your love, encouragement and support.

Special thanks to Jackie Arnot for writing on the Women In Ministry Fellowship wall on Facebook, to let me know that she would rather read what I was sharing in the form of a book in her hand. I believe the Father heard her request, hence, this book. Thank you to everyone who, subsequently, asked me to write this book!

Jennifer Abigail Lawson-Wallace

AUTHOR'S PREFACE

As a ministry, we have been called and mandated to strengthen and empower the Church, according to Ephesians 4:1-16. This has always been the focus of all that we do – discipling, teaching, training and equipping believers to know and walk with the Lord Jesus Christ, and releasing them to worship and serve Him.

However, as part of strengthening the Church, I also have a particular mandate from the Lord to raise and empower women to serve Him. Jesus Christ is coming soon; there is an urgent need for preparation, and the Gospel must be preached in every nation on the earth before He comes. (Matthew 24:14).

What we now have is a critical situation of 'all hands-on-deck'. Therefore, women must be restored, raised and released to work.

THE LORD NEEDS LABOURERS

Matthew 9:36-38 NKJV

"[36] But when He saw the multitudes, He was moved with compassion for them, because they were weary and scattered, like sheep having no shepherd. [37] Then He said to His disciples, "The harvest truly is plentiful, but the laborers are few. [38] Therefore pray the Lord of the harvest to send out laborers into His harvest.""

Jesus Christ bemoaned the fact that "the harvest is plentiful, but the labourers are few." The need for labourers cannot be over emphasised, and all hands must be on deck, for the Church to fulfil her assignment.

Unfortunately, however, many of the 'labourers' are sitting right in our churches, bound externally by culture and tradition, and internally by church doctrine; hindered from serving the Lord, simply because they are women!

A PROPHETIC CALL TO WOMEN

Psalm 68:11-12 TPT

"[11] God Almighty declares the word of the gospel with power, and the warring women of

> *Zion deliver its message: [12] "The conquering legions have themselves been conquered. Look at them flee!" Now Zion's women are left to gather the spoils."*

What is most incredible, however, is that God is indicating that women shall play a special role in the final harvest of souls into His Kingdom.

In his book, **"Why Not Women,"** the late Jamie Cunningham, founder of YWAM, spoke of the great benefits of sending women to the mission field. To him, the capacity, tenacity and efficiency of women on the mission field is incomparable. Ed Silvoso also discussed this in his book, *"Women, God's Secret Weapon."*

Women form the larger percentage of most congregations worldwide, and if they were properly discipled and released to work (not just as singers, stewards and Sunday School teachers in their churches, but out there in the harvest-field), the labour shortage would be reversed.

God is seeking to raise labourers, and is reaching out especially to women, since they form the majority in our churches, and because of their exceptionally unique God-given characteristics and ability to multiply, birth and nurture life.

This is the purpose for writing this book on the uniqueness of woman. My aim is to bring knowledge and revelation to women about their uniqueness and inherent God-given strength and capacity.

I am trusting that the truths revealed in this book would strengthen and encourage women to rise up wherever they are, in the knowledge of the power of God inherent in them, to be used by Him to reach out to their families, communities, societies and nations.

I also would like to help leaders realise, appreciate and utilise the untapped potential of the women who sit in their churches, week after week.

By doing do, we shall have the entire Body of Christ working effectively to fulfil the Great Commission.

Ephesians 4:16 TPT

"For his "body" has been formed in his image and is closely joined together and constantly connected as one. And every member has been given divine gifts to contribute to the growth of all; and as these gifts operate

> ***effectively throughout the whole body, we are built up and made perfect in love."***

The Body of Christ would then function as a whole and healthy body, with every part working effectively together to fulfil God's purpose. No one would be exempt or side-lined.

Jennifer Abigail Lawson-Wallace
CEO, Women In Tune

CHAPTER ONE

A WORLD WITHOUT WOMEN

"Picture and think of a world without women. Use your imagination, think outside the box. Describe what the world would be like if the woman had not been created or women ceased to exist. Consider all aspects of life, including family, society, economy, church, etc. What would the world be like, if women did not exist?"

This is an exercise we do with the women who attend our Discovering Identity and Purpose Training. The aim of the exercise is to encourage women to reflect and discover their worth and purpose, by examining what the world would be like if God had not created the woman.

ONCE UPON A TIME

The truth of the matter is that, once upon a time, women did not exist, and God thought that was not good enough!

> **Genesis 2:18,20 NASBS**
> *"[18] Then the LORD God said, "It is not good for the man to be alone; I will make him a helper suitable for him." [20] The man gave names to all the cattle, and to the birds of the sky, and to every beast of the field, but for Adam there was not found a helper suitable for him."*

Picture it.... The entire Creation had been spoken forth into manifestation by God; the earth, sea, sun, moon, stars, mountains, hills, trees, birds, beasts, rivers, streams, etc, had all been created. At the end of each day and phase of the process of creation, God had expressed His delight and pleasure... **and God saw that it was good!**

God had also created the man (male) in His image and likeness and given him the place of authority over the creation. However, the man abided alone, and for the first time in the entire process of creation, God expressed displeasure and He declared, ***"It is not good for the man to be alone!"*** The woman had not yet been created, and her absence would not serve God's purpose for creation!

IT DOES NOT SERVE GOD'S PURPOSE!

Many cultures and cultural practices degrade and relegate women; many consider women as subordinate and insignificant. Sadly, these views are also prevalent in the Church and have caused many women to not truly discovered their full value, purpose, position and potential in Christ.

This does not serve God's purpose, because it has caused the Church (in many nations) to operate under-capacity by limiting and under-utilizing the gifts, talents, abilities and callings of women! This has created a major setback to the fulfilment of the Great Commission, because in relegating women, the Church has inadvertently made more than half of God's workforce redundant.

The simple truth, however, is that just as a world without women would not serve God's purpose in the beginning, a Church that that does not regard and empower women and give them their rightful place in

Christ, would not fully serve or fulfil God's purpose.

BUT WHY?

Why is that so? What is so unique about the woman, that the scriptures are careful to describe what transpired prior to her creation, and how God made her an important and integral part of the creation story?

What made the woman so unique and different from everything else that God ever created? To discover this, is to discover the uniqueness of the Church, the Bride of Christ! *Think about it*!!!

WOMAN IS UNIQUE

> **Psalm 139:14 TPT**
>
> *"I thank you, God, for making me so mysteriously complex! Everything you do is marvellously breath-taking. It simply amazes me to think about it! How thoroughly you know me, Lord!*

The simple truth is that the woman is unique among all of God's creation.

- The word 'unique' is defined as *"Being the only existing one of its type."* It means to be unusual, peculiar or special in some way. Other definitions of unique are, *"to be distinct, exceptional, one of a kind and irreplaceable."* To be unique is to be authentic, genuine, real and original.

These are words that we must have in mind when we think of the uniqueness of woman. What makes woman exceptional, one of a kind and irreplaceable and different from everything else that God created?

It is true that man is also unique, but the sole focus of this book is the uniqueness of woman; in order to help the Church to understand the urgent need to strengthen and empower women to serve the Lord.

We do not have to travel far to discover the uniqueness of woman, as God in His awesome wisdom indicated that in the scriptures. The Book of Genesis Chapters One, Two and Three give several clear and valid indications of the exclusive, distinct, incomparable, one-of-a-kind nature of woman. So, join me on this exciting journey to discover what the scriptures have to say about the uniqueness of woman.

- **For Further Reading:** *Genesis Chapters 1, 2 and 3*

FOR REFLECTION

- Picture and think of a world without women. Use your imagination, think outside the box.

Describe what the world would be like if the woman had not been created or women ceased to exist. Consider all aspects of life, including family, society, economy, church, etc. What would the world be like, if women did not exist?

CHAPTER TWO

WOMAN IS A HUMAN BEING

Genesis 1:26-27 NKJV

"[26] Then God said, "Let Us make man in Our image, according to Our likeness; let them have dominion over the fish of the sea, over the birds of the air, and over the cattle, over all the earth and over every creeping thing that creeps on the earth." [27] So God created man in His own image; in the image of God He created him; male and female He created them."

The first thing that differentiates woman from the rest of the creation and makes her unique is that, together with man, she was created in God's image as a human being.

This makes woman different and distinct from the rest of creation - the sun, moon, trees, plants, animals, birds, etc. *(Genesis 2:18-20)*

A MERE RIB?

Now, this might seem strange to some, but there are cultural groups on this planet, that do not regard women as human beings. As I have travelled up and down the nations, I have heard some incredulous stories about the identity of woman.

One particular tribe, we were told, believes that a woman is not a human being; she is merely a rib taken out of man's side. Believe it or not, even pastors teach this to their congregations!

As a matter of fact, in one tribe in Africa, when a woman has a baby, the question is often asked, *"Did she have a human being or a girl?"* Implying that boys are human beings and girls are not.

Other tribes believe that a woman is merely a man's dog, making her subordinate to man, and part of his property. The general belief, however, is that women are part of the animals that God created.

Unfortunately, many of these cultural beliefs are also entrenched in the Church in these nations, so women are treated no differently from what the culture says or dictates. We have even come across bibles in local dialects, with certain verses removed to uphold the cultural beliefs about women!

MAN AND WOMAN = HUMANITY

This is why it is very important to establish, right from the beginning of our discussion, that the woman was created by God, as part of mankind, making her a human being.

> **Genesis 5:1-2 NKJV**
> *"[1] This is the book of the genealogy of Adam. In the day that God created man, He made him in the likeness of God. [2] He created them male and female, and blessed them and called them Mankind in the day they were created."*

Both scriptures mentioned above, Genesis 1:26-27 and Genesis 5:1-2, identify and establish humanity as male and female created in the image of God. Together with man, woman was uniquely created to reflect the image and likeness of God on the earth.

This provides evidence of woman's equality with man, because right at creation, God made them both equal in His likeness and image.

UNIQUE CHARACTERISTICS

One of the things that distinguish the woman as a human being, is that she was created in the image and likeness of God. As such, she was created as a spirit being, with a soul, dwelling in a body; just like her male counterpart.

> **I Thessalonians 5:23 NLT**
> *"Now may the God of peace make you holy in every way, and may your whole spirit and soul and body be kept blameless until our Lord Jesus Christ comes again."*

Together with man, woman was created as a human being, composed of *Spirit, Soul and Body*. This means that they both possessed the following characteristics and abilities:

1. They had the capacity to give and receive love.

2. They had the faculties of conscience, understanding, will and emotion.

    - Once upon a time, it was believed that the capacity of the average male brain was significantly greater than that of a female brain, making women less intelligent than men. Fortunately, science and history have proved that wrong. Women have an equal capacity to think, understand, learn and make decisions. Women have a will and the ability to exercise it. Women have emotions, which they can express at will.

3. They had the power and place of authority over the Creation.

   - As human beings, both man and woman were given power and the place of authority over the Creation.

     Genesis 1:26-28 NKJV

     "[26] Then God said, "Let Us make man in Our image, according to Our likeness; let them have dominion over the fish of the sea, over the birds of the air, and over the cattle, over all the earth and over every creeping thing that creeps on the earth." [27] So God created man in His own image; in the image of God He created him; male and female He created them."

- God gave both of them the authority and power to govern and exercise dominion; thus, raising them both above Creation.

4. They had purity and goodness, and were righteous before God.

Genesis 2:25 NKJV
"And they were both naked, the man and his wife, and were not ashamed."

- As human beings created in the image of God, both man and woman possessed purity and goodness and a right standing with God. Prior to their sin, they were both holy and righteous before God. They each had a relationship with God and could communicate with Him.

These characteristics are unique and not found in the rest of creation, only in humanity. These characteristics are what make both men and women unique human beings, and clearly differentiate them from the rest of the Creation.

EQUAL, DIFFERENT & INTERDEPENDENT

As human beings, we project the image of God as male and female, since God is male-female in His totality. Any balanced projection of God, therefore, must include both the male and the female aspects.

> **Genesis 5:1-2 NLT**
> *"[1] This is the written account of the descendants of Adam. When God created human beings, he made them to be like himself. [2] He created them male and female, and he blessed them and called them "human.""*

Thus, the scriptures provide evidence of woman's humanity, as well as her equality with man. God made them both in His likeness and image as **equal, different and interdependent.**

EQUAL

Man and woman are equal. Despite the controversy, there is no suggestion in the Creation story that man is better than or superior to woman. They were both created in the image of God and reflect what exists within the Godhead. The Father, the Son and the Holy Spirit are all equally GOD, in nature, constitution, essence, glory and power. Man, woman and their offspring are all human beings.

DIFFERENT

Although the man and the woman were created in God's image as are equal human beings, they are not the same.

Man and woman are two different and separate parts of a whole. They are designed differently and function differently from each other, in order to fulfil one purpose. This reflects the Godhead, where, God the Father, the Son and Holy Spirit, all being equally God, perform different functions to fulfil one purpose.

The differences between men and women are discussed in-depth in my book "DESIGNED FOR PURPOSE: Woman Fearfully and Wonderfully Made" *(Also, see Page 83 for a summary of the differences).*

INTERDEPENDENT

God created man and woman to be interdependent on each other. Man and woman share a common goal and purpose, to be fruitful and multiply, and exercise dominion over the earth; which they would never fulfil independently of each other.

This is a true reflection of the Godhead, where God the Father, the Son and the Holy Spirit are interdependent on each other, to fulfil their divine purpose. As human beings, created in God's image, man and woman need to be interdependent on each other.

This is why God created the marriage institution, to bind them together and make them one.

ADAM'S AFFIRMATION

Another sign of the woman's uniqueness as a human being, was how Adam instantly recognised, acknowledged and affirmed her!

Genesis 2:23 NKJV

"And Adam said: "This is now bone of my bones and flesh of my flesh; she shall be called Woman, because she was taken out of Man.""

Prior to that, God had given Adam a chance to search throughout all the Creation to see if he could find anything suitable for himself and to fulfil the task God had given him to do, but he had found nothing. However, Adam immediately recognised and acknowledged the woman as his counterpart and co-equal; whereas before, he could find none.

The man, Adam, endorsed woman's uniqueness as his counterpart; a fellow human being, with the same mandate, power and authority!

CHAPTER THREE

THE VACUUM

Genesis 2:18-20 AMP

"[18] Now the LORD God said, "It is not good (beneficial) for the man to be alone; I will make him a helper [one who balances him-a counterpart who is] suitable and complementary for him." [19] So the LORD God formed out of the ground every animal of the field and every bird of the air, and brought them to Adam to see what he would call them; and whatever the man called a living creature, that was its name. [20] And the man gave names to all the livestock, and to the birds of the air, and to every animal of the field; but for Adam there was not found a helper [that was] suitable (a companion) for him."

Another indication of the woman's uniqueness was the huge vacuum that existed before her creation.

Before woman was created, God declared that her non-existence was not good. Throughout the 'process' of creation, over and over again the Bible states, "And God saw that it was good." Then suddenly, for the first time, God did not only see, but declared, "It is not good..." SOMEONE very essential to fulfilling God's plans and purposes was still missing.

All of Creation was in place – the sun, moon, galaxies, mountains, hills, trees, plants, animals, birds, fishes, etc, had all been created and assigned their place and purpose on the earth. Yet, man, with his important God-given assignment to take dominion over the earth and to multiply and replenish it, was all alone and by himself.

There was absolutely nothing in the entire Creation to substitute or replace that which was missing. God's plans and purpose for Creation stood at a crossroads. Something had to be done urgently!

Was this an error on God's part? Did He forget or miss something? Many have said that woman was created as an afterthought, to rectify a problem with Creation. This cannot be true of God as that would greatly undermine God's omniscience. Does God not know the end of a matter from its beginning? *(Isaiah 46:10)*.

God is constant and consistent, the same yesterday, today and forever. He is all-knowing, and with Him there is no shadow of turning; neither does He make mistakes.

The seeming delay in the creation of the woman was an essential part of the divine plan to show the man the value of the woman, above all Creation. The fact that there was a lack of an appropriate replacement for woman in all of Creation clearly indicates her uniqueness, essence and value. There was nothing or no one in all of Creation quite like her.

The big vacuum and gaping hole in Creation and man's life spoke very loudly and clearly when God Himself said, "IT IS NOT GOOD!"

It was only after both man and woman had been created and commissioned that God looked upon everything He had created, saw that it was all good, and then He rested.

INDEED, A WORLD WITHOUT WOMEN WOULD CREATE A HUGE VACUUM AND NEVER SERVE GOD'S PURPOSE! WOMEN ARE AS EQUALLY IMPORTANT AS MEN, AND AS MUCH NEEDED BY GOD, TO FULFIL HIS PURPOSES!

CHAPTER FOUR

THE METHOD OF HER CREATION

Psalm 139:14 NLT

"Thank you for making me so wonderfully complex! Your workmanship is marvellous-how well I know it."

A further indication of woman's uniqueness is the method by which God created her. We have already established that both man and woman were created, in God's image, differently from the rest of Creation. However, the method of the creation of the man was evidently different from that of the woman.

Although they were both were created in God's image, they were created differently. The very method and process of her creation distinguished the woman from the man and everything else.

THE CREATION OF THE MAN

Genesis 2:7 AMP

"Then the LORD God formed [that is, created the body of] man from the dust of the ground, and breathed into his nostrils the breath of life; and the man became a living being [an individual complete in body and spirit]."

With the creation of the man, the Bible tells us that God took dust and FORMED man out of the dust, breathed life into him and man came alive.

The Hebrew word for 'formed' is *'yatsar'* (pronounced yaw-tsar), which means to form, fashion or frame. It also means to preordain, pre-determine, plan or give purpose to a situation.

- *'Yatsar'* gives a notion of an initial sketch, outline or drawing, similar to the initial sketch an artist makes before actually filling a painting with colour and detail, or the structure/frame a builder puts up before actually laying the bricks, pipes, etc.

THE CREATION OF THE WOMAN

With the creation of woman, however, the method and process were entirely different.

> **Genesis 2:21-22 AMP**
> *"[21] And the Lord God caused a deep sleep to fall upon Adam; and while he slept, He took one of his ribs or a part of his side and closed up the [place with] flesh. [22] And the rib or part of his side, which the Lord God had taken from the man, He built up and made into a woman, and He brought her to the man."*

First of all, God put Adam to sleep. Whilst he was sleeping, God took out one of his ribs and closed up the place with flesh. Then, with the rib that He had taken out of man, God fashioned, built up and made woman! This was totally different from how He created the man.

- The Hebrew word for 'MADE' is *'banah'* {pronounced baw-naw} which means to build, setup, build up a family; to establish and cause to continue, to make permanent. The word 'build' has a connotation of the process involved in building a house, based on architectural design, giving attention to detail and plan.

- This indicates that whereas the creation of man was of a 'temporary' nature, the creation of woman gave permanence, stability and structure. This explains why God had said' "It is not good that the man should be alone!" The man was an unfinished creation!

- All great artists make a rough draft before they make a masterpiece. Our God of great wisdom, in creating humanity, first 'drew' a sketch of the man, with every intention of completing him by bringing the woman alongside to add detail, structure, beauty and permanence, and thus build up humanity.

No wonder King Solomon that said, *"He who finds a wife a finds a good thing and obtains favour from the Lord"* (Proverbs 18:22)

CHAPTER FIVE

A HELP MEET FOR MAN

One of the most misquoted, abused and misunderstood, scriptures in the Bible is Genesis 2:18. Often quoted from the King James Version, it says,

> *"And the Lord God said, It is not good that the man should be alone; I will make him an HELPMEET for him."*

With this single translation of the Bible, and one word, "helpmeet," many have relegated women to a subservient and subordinate position, in relationship to men.

To many, women were simply created to serve men. Actually, one pastor told me that women were created to be in the kitchen, to cook, clean wash and iron clothes, and take care of their men and children.

Which makes me ask the question:

> *"Was it because Adam, the first man, had no one to cook for him, or clean and iron his clothes that God said, "It is not good for the man to be alone?""*

OF COURSE NOT! Bearing in mind that the man was naked and so had no clothes, did not need to cook his food and had no children to be taken care of!

Obviously, the man lacked something or someone; but what was lacking or what did he need help with? The answer to the question should give us a further clue about the uniqueness of woman. God had promised him a help meet, a helper comparable to him.

EZER KENEDGO

In the original English translation of the Bible, KJV, two words were joined as one "helpmeet," to describe the woman.

However, in the Hebrew, "help meet" are two separate words:

1. "Ezer"
2. "Kenegdo"

EZER:

The Jewish interpretation of the term "ezer," is "helper." It is often used in the scriptures to describe God as an intervener, deliverer, shield and helper of His people.

- *'Ezer'* appears twenty-one times in the Old Testament - twice in reference to Eve, three times in reference to nations to whom Israel appealed for military support, and sixteen times in reference to God as the helper of Israel. None of these references suggest weakness, inferiority, or subserviency; on the contrary, they suggest ability, strength and power.

I Samuel 7:12 NLT

"Samuel then took a large stone and placed it between the towns of Mizpah and Jeshanah. He named it EBENEZER (which means "the stone of help"), for he said, "Up to this point the LORD has helped us!""

- *'Ezer'* simply means "to help," and implies compassion, generosity and strength. Ezer is a popular name for

Jewish boys both in biblical and in modern times.

THE HOLY SPIRIT

John 14:26 NKJV

"But the HELPER, the Holy Spirit, whom the Father will send in My name, He will teach you all things, and bring to your remembrance all things that I said to you."

Jesus described the Holy Spirit as our Helper, sent from the Father to be with us, transform us, and strengthen and empower us to fulfil the task of the Great Commission.

This should tell us a great deal about the woman, the helper, created in the image and likeness of God, with the nature, capacity and strength needed by the man to fulfil the purpose of being fruitful, multiplying and replenishing the earth and taking dominion over it.

- **For Further Reading:** *Genesis 1:26-28; Genesis 2*

KENEGDO

'Kenegdo' is translated as "meet, befitting or appropriate." It literally means "as in front of him," suggesting that the "EZER" that God was creating would be the perfect match for the man; "a helper like himself," a counterpart, or a corresponding character.

- One thing we can be sure of, is that, God had created the man in His image, likeness and glory; He was certainly not going to create his wife of a lesser image, likeness and glory. If they are to reproduce after kind, they must be a perfect match; they must compliment and correspond to each other in nature, essence, glory and authority.

- In the Hebrew, "help meet," therefore, is not just *'ezer,'* but *'ezer k'gnedo,'* which means "the help that opposes." The Rabbis explain this term as two posts of equal weight leaned against each other. They stand upright because of equal force and strength. *(See diagram on the next page).*

A help meet – a perfect match - a helper like himself, of corresponding character and nature)

REPRODUCTIVE CAPACITY OF WOMAN

Genesis 1:28 NKJV

[28] Then God blessed them, and God said to them, "Be fruitful and multiply; fill the earth and subdue it; have dominion over the fish of the sea, over the birds of the air, and over every living thing that moves on the earth."

The one thing that distinguishes women from men is their reproductive capacity. Women were designed and created to receive, multiply and bring forth life. Everything a woman takes, she multiplies, births and nurtures.

Give a wife love and she will multiply it and give you back a marriage and home filled with love, peace, joy, fruitfulness and happiness. Give wife insults and she will give you back a home filled with pain, sorrow, unhappiness and no peace.

Although the man had seed in his loins, he could never reproduce his seed by himself. He was incapable of doing that because he had not been created with the organs, strength and ability to do so. Therefore, one of the things that made the woman the perfect *"ezer kenegdo"* for the man was her reproductive ability and capacity. God created her with all the necessary apparatus, capacity and strength to reproduce.

This was just what Adam needed and was lacking – someone with the ability, capability and capacity to multiply, travail, nurture, reproduce, bring forth, birth and raise life. Without such a person, the man would never fulfil God's purpose of reproducing and replenishing the earth, and taking dominion over it.

Therefore, a world without woman would eventually cause the entire human race to be wiped out! This is what makes her a unique help meet for man. Yes, women are unique, like that!

CHAPTER SIX

HER TIME ALONE WITH GOD

Genesis 2:21-22 AMP
"[21] So the LORD God caused a deep sleep to fall upon Adam; and while he slept, He took one of his ribs and closed up the flesh at that place. [22] And the rib which the LORD God had taken from the man He made (fashioned, formed) into a woman, and He brought her and presented her to the man."

Another evidence of the uniqueness of the woman is the time she spent alone with God, throughout the process of her creation.

It is interesting to note that God denied the man the privilege of seeing or getting involved with the creation of the woman. The man was simply not included; rather God caused a deep sleep to come upon him, and as he slept, the LORD created the woman.

Thus, God distinguished His relationship with the woman by spending time alone with her whilst the man slept. God valued her individuality and endorsed it the same way in which He had endorsed the man's, before woman was created. Whilst the man slept, all of creation stood still and watched, as God fashioned and built His unique and priceless creation, Woman!

Therefore, she did not have to relate with God through the man, nor did not have to access God through the man. She had her own personal relationship with Him!

THE BIRTH OF JESUS

The story of the birth of Jesus seems to endorse the fact of woman's individuality, especially, in her relationship with God. The angel Gabriel was sent to a woman named Mary, who was betrothed to a man named Joseph, to inform her of the role she would play in the birth of our Saviour Jesus.

Her husband, Joseph, was not consulted; in fact, he was completely out of the picture on that occasion, as the angel discussed the details with Mary. In response, Mary made an independent decision to accept God's plan for her life.

WE ALL HAVE ACCESS

Many women think it is through their husbands that they can gain acceptance from God or serve Him. Others have embraced the false teaching that their husbands are their priests. There is no scripture to endorse this teaching; it is a fallacy.

We have all been given access to God, which is an essential privilege of our royal priesthood. Access to God is by the finished work of the Cross and Blood of Jesus Christ, not by gender. Jesus, our High Priest, has given us access!

TO THE SINGLE WOMAN:

Never let the absence of a man in your life hinder you from getting close to God, and knowing and walking with Him. Seize the day, and develop and enjoy your relationship and fellowship with Him. This is what you were uniquely and specially created for.

TO THE MARRIED WOMAN:

Never let being married take you away from your time alone with the God; focus on Him, and take time apart to develop and deepen your relationship and fellowship with the Lord. Certainly, this is what you were uniquely and specially created for. AMEN!!!

- **For Further Reading:** *Luke 1; Galatians 3:26-28; Hebrews 4:15-16*

CHAPTER SEVEN

THE MAN'S RECOGNITION

Genesis 2:23 NLT

""At last!" the man exclaimed. "This one is bone from my bone, and flesh from my flesh! She will be called 'woman,' because she was taken from 'man.'"

With this powerful declaration, the man recognised the woman, affirmed her uniqueness and endorsed her as his counterpart!

"Yes! This one is just like me and corresponds to me! She is my counterpart!!!"

Remember, that God had given Adam the chance to search through all Creation to see if he could find someone, something or anything suitable, befitting and appropriate for himself and the task that God had given him to fulfil; but he had found nothing.

There was nothing in the entire Creation that equalled him or could stand together with him, as his counterpart. God stepped in to unveil one of His choicest, glorious creations, the WOMAN; to be the perfect companion for His other choicest, glorious creation, the MAN!

Adam woke up and, suddenly, there she was; everything he ever wanted or needed! Thus, he declared, *"This is what I have been waiting for… Bone of my bone and flesh of my flesh!"* Adam immediately recognised and acknowledged the woman as his co-equal and counterpart, whereas before, he could find none.

BONE FROM BONE, FLESH FROM FLESH

> ***"This one is bone from my bone, and flesh from my flesh!"***

What a statement! What a declaration! What an endorsement and affirmation from the man! They were one and the same! They differed from the rest of the Creation, but they were one and the same. They were the same human flesh, carrying God's nature, essence and glory.

Jesus Christ reminded us that this declaration and affirmation is the very foundation of the institution of marriage; that the man and the woman are not different and separate, but one and the same flesh and bone!

Matthew 19:4-6 NKJV

"[4] And He answered and said to them, "Have you not read that He who made them at the beginning 'made them male and female,' [5] and said, 'For this reason a man shall leave his father and mother and be joined to his wife, and the two shall become ONE FLESH'? [6] So then, they are no longer two but one flesh. Therefore, what God has joined together, let not man separate.""

YODH HEY

"She will be called 'woman,' because she was taken from 'man.'"

The man named this latest creation of God, "woman." In the Hebrew, man is ***"Ish"*** and woman is ***"Ishshah"***

When the two names are written in Hebrew, the difference between them is that "man" has the letter "YOHD" and woman has the letter "HEY". When these two names are put together, it spells "YOHD HEY," which is, YAH, the poetic form of God's name.

This confirms that the man and the woman were the same; both created in the image and likeness of God. Each of them has a piece of the name of God, but only when they come together as one flesh, can we see the Creator's name, nature, essence, authority and glory manifested. *Remember, that they were created as equal, different and interdependent.*

It takes both the male and the female to display the image of God in the earth. This is why God needs both men and women, in marriage and in the Church, to fulfil His plans and purposes on the earth. SELAH!!!

- **For Further Reading:** *Genesis 2:18-25; Ephesians 5:22-33; Matthew 19:4-5*

CHAPTER EIGHT

A DIFFERENT JUDGEMENT

Even in judgement, God differentiated between the man and the woman! Unfortunately, Adam and Eve rebelled against God by listening to the serpent, the devil, and God dealt with their sin by pronouncing judgement on all parties involved – the serpent, the woman and man. However, the woman's judgement was clearly different from that of the man.

Together, their sentence was death and eternal separation from God; however, individually, the man and the woman received specific judgements for their sin.

- To the woman, God said,

> *"I will greatly multiply your sorrow and your conception; in pain you shall bring forth children; your desire shall be for your husband, and he shall rule over you."* [Genesis 3:16 NKJV]

- However, to the Man, God said,

> *"[17b] ...Cursed is the ground for your sake; In toil you shall eat of it all the days of your life. [18] Both thorns and thistles it shall bring forth for you, and you shall eat the herb of the field. [19] In the sweat of your face you shall eat bread till you return to the ground, for out of it you were taken; for dust you are, and to dust you shall return."* [Genesis 3:17b-19 NKJV]

Both man and woman were judged, but differently, and in accordance with their purpose, makeup and function. Thus, this unfortunate situation revealed a further uniqueness and difference between man and woman.

THE SERPENT'S JUDGEMENT

One of the strongest indications of the woman's uniqueness is found in God's judgement to the serpent, after Adam and Eve had sinned. In His sentence to the serpent, God outlined His redemptive and restorative plan for humanity, and provided a crucial indicator to the exceptional nature and essence of woman.

> **Genesis 3:15 NASBS**
> *"And I will put enmity between you and the woman, and between your seed and her seed; he shall bruise you on the head, and you shall bruise him on the heel."*

In His judgement, God promised Satan that there would be a blood feud between him and the woman, and she would be his worst enemy; the woman and her seed would bring him down and destroy him. The Sovereign Almighty God placed the responsibility of redemption, deliverance, restoration, reconciliation and overcoming the enemy upon the woman and her seed.

The major part of this promise has been fulfilled through Jesus Christ, the Seed of woman. Jesus, whose human DNA carries only that of a woman, crushed the head of Satan when He defeated him on the Cross. Through Christ, humanity has been redeemed and can be reconciled with God.

Yet, there is more to this promise; women would rise up in the power of Jesus Christ to fight against the works of darkness.

I believe that is one of the major reasons why the enemy has sought and worked hard to keep women bound, abused and oppressed for centuries.

WHY WOMEN?

The question is, why would God say such a thing? Why the woman and not the man, or both of them? What is so peculiar about the woman that God would place such a responsibility upon her? The truth is that God created woman in His image with an inherent strength and wisdom to overcome the enemy. This is what further defines our uniqueness!

> *"...From now on you and the woman will be enemies"* (TLB).

> *"...I'm declaring war between you and the Woman"* (TM).

> *"...And I will cause hostility between you and the woman"* (NLT).

- Indeed, God is stirring up anger in women against the enemy. Women, blood-bought and washed, Spirit-filled and on fire for Jesus, are going to rise up with a God-given anger against the works of evil in their nations. Hallelujah!

THE CHURCH

In this aspect is the Church, the Bride of Christ, victorious; because to discover the uniqueness of woman is to further discover the uniqueness of the Church, the Bride of Christ. As women discover and exhibit the nature of God in them, the Church will begin to manifest that very nature.

The Church (especially women) shall rise up in anger and fight against the works of evil in our home, families, communities, villages, towns, cities, nations and the whole world. We shall demonstrate to the principalities and powers that Jesus is Lord. *(Ephesians 3:10)*.

We shall rise up and proclaim the glorious gospel of Jesus Christ, starting from our homes, through our communities, societies and nations, to the uttermost part of the world.

Psalm 68:11-12 TPT

"[11] God Almighty declares the word of the gospel with power, and the warring women of Zion deliver its message: [12] "The conquering legions have themselves been conquered. Look at them flee!" Now Zion's women are left to gather the spoils."

AMEN AND AMEN!!!

CHAPTER NINE

THE MOTHER OF ALL LIVING

Genesis 3:20 AMP

"The man named his wife Eve (life spring, life giver), because she was the mother of all the living."

After God passed judgement, the scripture says that the man changed the woman's name, and called her by the name, 'Eve' (Hebrew 'Chavvah'), which means 'life-giver' or 'life-spring.'

Remember, when he first met her, he named her "woman," because she came out of him. *(Genesis 2:23)*. What was it that prompted Adam to change the woman's name from "Woman" to "Chavvah" (Eve)? What did Adam hear that brought hope and prompted him to declare the woman as the life-spring of humanity?

The merciful God had declared hope in His judgement. Through the woman and her offspring, Jesus Christ, humanity shall be redeemed and restored. Yes, the woman had been declared the life-spring of humanity, one who births and nurtures life, the MOTHER OF ALL THE LIVING. No one else, in all the Creation, received this name and title but the woman, indicating her uniqueness!

Indeed, woman is the mother of all the living; the gateway for all mankind to enter the world, including Jesus Christ the Messiah.

WOMEN WHO BIRTHED THE SEED

It is interesting to note that throughout the bible, whenever the Seed of the Messiah faced extinction, God always found a woman through whom He would bring forth and preserve the seed.

Let's look at some of the women that God used to preserve the Seed Who destroy Satan and give life to all humanity.

1. EVE

Upon careful reading and studying of the bible, one realises that Eve took God's promise to the serpent seriously and watched over it, expecting its fulfilment. We see this through her excitement at the birth of her sons, and the names she gave them.

CAIN

Genesis 4:1 NASBS

"Now the man had relations with his wife Eve, and she conceived and gave birth to Cain, and she said, "I HAVE GOTTEN A MANCHILD WITH THE HELP OF THE LORD.""

God had promised redemption and restoration through her seed, so Eve named her first son, Cain, which means *"acquired or possessed."* Eve's expectation was expressed when she declared that, with the help of the LORD, she had acquired a manchild, a son. Despite the consequences and effects of their sin, it is evident that Eve had strong faith in God's word and promise.

ABEL

Genesis 4:2 NASBS

"Again, she gave birth to his brother Abel. And

Abel was a keeper of flocks, but Cain was a tiller of the ground."

After the birth of Cain, Eve conceived again and named him, Abel, which means, *"breath,"* the source of life. Eve was hopeful and expectant that God would bring deliverance through her sons, and Abel was righteous and found favour with God.

Unfortunately, however, SIN, now unleashed, was lurking around. Out of jealousy, Cain killed his brother; simply because God accepted Abel's sacrifice and rejected his! Cain was cursed by God, and Eve lost both sons.

Yet, she did not lose hope! She conceived again and brought forth another son, Seth. Could this be the promised seed?

SETH

Genesis 4:25-26 NKJV

"[25] And Adam knew his wife again, and she bore a son and named him Seth, "FOR GOD HAS APPOINTED ANOTHER SEED FOR ME instead of Abel, whom Cain killed." [26] And as for Seth, to him also a son was born; and

he named him Enosh. THEN MEN BEGAN TO CALL ON THE NAME OF THE LORD."

Eve named her third son Seth, which means, *'compensation.'* With hope, and in earnest expectation, she declared that God had appointed and given her another righteous seed, instead of Abel, the one she lost. It was through Seth's offspring Enosh, that people began to call on the name of the LORD.

2. SARAH

In seeking to redeem and restore humanity, God found a faithful man, Abraham, and promised to make him the father of all nations; in him all the nations of the earth would be blessed. This promise was made to Abraham and his seed, not seeds. (Galatians 3:16).

However, Sarah, Abraham's wife was barren, old and gone past menopause. God made a covenant with Abraham; and God included Sarah in His covenant promise to Abraham...!

Genesis 17:16-19 NKJV

"[16] And I will bless her and also give you a son by her; then I will bless her, and she shall be a mother of nations; kings of peoples shall be from her." [17] Then Abraham fell on his face and laughed, and said in his heart, "Shall a child be born to a man who is one hundred years old? And shall Sarah, who is ninety years old, bear a child?" [18] And Abraham said to God, "Oh, that Ishmael might live before You!" [19] Then God said: "No, Sarah your wife shall bear you a son, and you shall call his name Isaac; I will establish My covenant with him for an everlasting covenant, and with his descendants after him."

Sarah was barren, old and gone past menopause; nevertheless, at the word of God, she conceived and brought forth Isaac, a type of Christ.

Hebrews 11:11 TPT

"Sarah's faith embraced the miracle power to conceive even though she was barren and was past the age of childbearing, for the authority of her faith rested in the One who made the promise, and she tapped into his faithfulness."
AMEN!

3. REBEKAH

Over time, God passed on the promise of the redemption of the nations to Abraham and his Seed, and Sarah was chosen by God to birth Isaac, a type of Christ.

It was very important that the woman who carried the seed and continued the lineage should be the right one. Rebekah was chosen by divine orchestration, and as she was leaving her people to go and marry Isaac, they blessed her with the blessing of reproduction and dominion, which was originally given to Adam and Eve…

> **Genesis 24:60 NKJV**
>
> *"And they blessed Rebekah and said to her: "Our sister, may you become the mother of thousands of ten thousands; and may your descendants possess the gates of those who hate them.""*

Rebekah married Isaac, but struggled to conceive because she was barren. God opened her womb when Isaac prayed and interceded for her, and Rebekah conceived twins.

Genesis 25:22-23 NKJV

"[22] But the children struggled together within her; and she said, "If all is well, why am I like this?" So she went to inquire of the LORD. [23] And the LORD said to her: "Two nations are in your womb, two peoples shall be separated from your body; one people shall be stronger than the other, and the older shall serve the younger.""

God revealed to Rebekah that her younger son, Jacob, was His chosen seed. Rebekah watched over this word, and through careful planning and plotting, she ensured that the blessing of the seed did not go to the wrong son, Esau, but to Isaac, the one chosen by God.

Without Rebekah's intervention, Jacob would have passed on the blessing to Esau; contrary to God's word. Women are truly unique and when they are in tune and in partnership with God, great things happen, and His plans and purposes unfold and are fulfilled.

- **For Further Reading:** *Genesis 24; Genesis 25:19-28; Genesis 27:1-17*

4. TAMAR

The story of Tamar, an abandoned widow, can be found in Genesis 38.

Jacob, the son of Isaac, son of Abraham, had twelve sons; one of them, Judah was chosen to continue the lineage and produce the seed that would eventually birth the Messiah. Judah had three sons, two of whom got married to Tamar. Here's the story…

Genesis 38:6-11 NLT

"[6] In the course of time, Judah arranged for his firstborn son, Er, to marry a young woman named Tamar. [7] But Er was a wicked man in the LORD's sight, so the LORD took his life. [8] Then Judah said to Er's brother Onan, "Go and marry Tamar, as our law requires of the brother of a man who has died. You must produce an heir for your brother." [9] But Onan was not willing to have a child who would not be his own heir. So whenever he had intercourse with his brother's wife, he spilled the semen on the ground. This prevented her from having a child who would belong to his brother. [10] But the LORD considered it evil for Onan to deny a child to his dead brother. So the LORD took Onan's life, too. [11] Then

> *Judah said to Tamar, his daughter-in-law, "Go back to your parents' home and remain a widow until my son Shelah is old enough to marry you." (But Judah didn't really intend to do this because he was afraid Shelah would also die, like his two brothers.) So Tamar went back to live in her father's home."*

Tamar faced a possible permanent status of widowhood and childlessness, yet, she did not give up on taking seed! With the men failing to uphold the law, the lineage of Judah faced extinction without an heir.

Tamar took matters into her own hands, posed as a prostitute and tricked her father-in-law, Judah, into having sex with her, in order to produce a child for the lineage.

Thus, Tamar became pregnant by her father-in-law, and bore him twin sons - Perez and Zerah. The lineage of the Messiah was to pass through Judah to Perez, and onward.

Tamar's method was very unorthodox, but it gave her the children she longed for and a place of honour in history. Judah himself declared that Tamar was more righteous and honourable than him. Interestingly, the bible did not condemn her, but honoured her, by placing her among the men in the genealogy of Jesus Christ.

> **Matthew 1:3 NASBS**
> *"Judah was the father of Perez and Zerah by Tamar, Perez was the father of Hezron, and Hezron the father of Ram."*

Although she did not know it then, Tamar played an important role in continuing Judah's lineage, through which the Messiah would be born. Tamar took the seed by force and produced a son, an heir of God's promise of deliverance and redemption.

Question: How far would we go, as women, to preserve the seed of the Gospel of the Kingdom of Jesus Christ, in our nations. Selah!

- **For Further Reading:** *Genesis 38; Matthew 11:12*

5. JOCHEBED, THE MOTHER OF MOSES

> **Exodus 1:15-16,22 NLT**
> *"[15] Then Pharaoh, the king of Egypt, gave*

> *this order to the Hebrew midwives, Shiphrah and Puah: [16] "When you help the Hebrew women as they give birth, watch as they deliver. If the baby is a boy, kill him; if it is a girl, let her live." ...[22] Then Pharaoh gave this order to all his people: "Throw every newborn Hebrew boy into the Nile River. But you may let the girls live.""*

Once again, the seed of the Messiah faced extinction, as Pharaoh issued a decree that the seed of Israel should be exterminated – all new-born sons should be killed at birth. Yet again, God found a faithful woman, Jochabed, to preserve the seed and raise a deliverer for His people.

> **Exodus 2:1-2 NLT**
> *"[1] About this time, a man and woman from the tribe of Levi got married. [2] The woman became pregnant and gave birth to a son. She saw that he was a special baby and kept him hidden for three months."*

Then, Jochebed came up with a plan to save and deliver her son Moses' life. Together, with her daughter Miriam, they preserved the life of Moses and got him to be raised as a prince in Pharaoh's household. Moses became the deliverer of Israel, a type of Christ, the Seed of woman.

6. RUTH

The story of Ruth happened after the time of the Judges, one of the darkest periods in the history of Israel, when everybody did what was right in their own eyes.

> **Judges 21:25 NKJV**
> *"In those days there was no king in Israel; everyone did what was right in his own eyes."*

Ruth was a Moabite, a people highly detested by God. *(Deuteronomy 23:3).* Ruth was also a widow; however, she made a decision to follow Yahweh, the God of Israel. Under the guidance of Naomi, Ruth prepared herself; she washed and anointed herself, put on her best garments and went down to the threshing floor, in order to get Boaz to marry her.

> **Ruth 4:13-22 NKJV**
> *"[13] So Boaz took Ruth and she became his wife; and when he went in to her, the LORD*

> *gave her conception, and SHE BORE A SON. [14] Then the women said to Naomi, "Blessed be the LORD, who has not left you this day without a close relative; and may his name be famous in Israel! [15] And may he be to you a restorer of life and a nourisher of your old age; for your daughter-in-law, who loves you, who is better to you than seven sons, has borne him." [16] Then Naomi took the child and laid him on her bosom, and became a nurse to him. [17] Also the neighbour women gave him a name, saying, "There is a son born to Naomi." And they called his name Obed. He is the father of Jesse, the father of David. [18] Now this is the genealogy of Perez: Perez begot Hezron; [19] Hezron begot Ram, and Ram begot Amminadab; [20] Amminadab begot Nahshon, and Nahshon begot Salmon; [21] Salmon begot Boaz, and Boaz begot Obed; [22] Obed begot Jesse, and Jesse begot (King) David."*

Through the efforts of Naomi and Ruth, God raised a King for Israel and restored the lineage of the Seed of the Messiah. Ruth, a poor, Moabite widow, also gained a place of honour among the men in the genealogy of Jesus. Christ. *(Matthew 1:5)*

It is incredible that God chooses to use faithful ordinary women to accomplish His extraordinary plans.

- **For Further Reading:** *Exodus 2; The Book of Ruth*

7. OTHER WOMEN

Over the centuries, many women have fulfilled this title and role, as God has used them to preserve the lineage of the Messiah, who would redeem and humanity. So far, we have discussed Eve, Sarah, Rebekah, Tamar, Jochabed, and Ruth.

Other examples include Rachel, who in her barrenness cried out to Jacob, "Give me children, or else I die!" She birthed Joseph, who delivered Israel and the entire world from famine. Manoah' wife, took seed by divine mandate and birthed Samson, who delivered Israel from the hands of the Philistines.

Hannah's cry to God for a child was answered and she gave birth to Samuel, who would lead Israel in the ways of God.

Bathsheba birthed Solomon and helped establish him as King after his father David.

There were countless other unnamed, unmentioned and unacclaimed women who were also used by God to fulfil His judgement to the serpent. However, we cannot conclude this discussion without including Mary, the mother of Jesus.

8. MARY, THE MOTHER OF JESUS

Mary was a virgin betrothed to Joseph, when an angel appeared to inform her that she had been chosen to conceive and bear a Son by the Holy Spirit.

Luke 1:28-33 NKJV

"[28] And having come in, the angel said to her, "Rejoice, highly favored one, the Lord is with you; BLESSED ARE YOU AMONG WOMEN!" [29] But when she saw him, she was troubled at his saying, and considered what manner of greeting this was. [30] Then the angel said to her, "Do not be afraid, Mary, for you have found favor with God. [31] And behold, YOU SHALL CONCEIVE IN YOUR WOMB AND BRING FORTH A SON, and shall call His name JESUS. [32] He will be great,

and will be called the Son of the Highest; and the Lord God will give Him the throne of His father David. [33] And He will reign over the house of Jacob forever, and of His kingdom there will be no end.""

Mary's life suddenly got overwhelmingly out of her control. All her plans and aspirations were suddenly overturned by the angel's announcement. Her future suddenly became uncertain.

She faced a possible scandal, public ridicule and the prospect of being stoned to death for being pregnant out of wedlock. What would Joseph say? What would people say? Yet, Mary submitted to God's will…

Luke 1:38 NKJV

"Then Mary said, "Behold the maidservant of the Lord! Let it be to me according to your word…"

- Mary took the Seed from God and gave birth to Jesus Christ, the promised Messiah, Redeemer and Saviour of the world. He died a cruel and shameful death on the cross, rose from the dead and ascended back to heaven to reconcile humanity with God.

In these perilous times, when the Kingdom of Jesus Christ faces enormous challenges in the nations, God is still looking for women who would travail and birth the seeds of righteousness, peace and joy in our nations. Every one of us is eligible in Christ! YES, WOMEN ARE UNIQUE, LIKE THAT!!!

- **For Further Reading:** *Genesis 30:1, 22-24; Judges 13; 1 Samuel 1; Luke 1*

CHAPTER TEN

PURPOSE DETERMINES DESIGN

It is said that the purpose of a thing determines its design; therefore, to fully understand the uniqueness of woman and her purpose, we must look at the way God designed her to function.

Romans 1:20 NKJV

"For since the creation of the world His invisible attributes are clearly seen, being understood by the things that are made, even His eternal power and Godhead"

The woman was created in the image and likeness of God. Though God is unseen, He reveals Himself and His attributes through His creation. God's nature is entwined into every facet of our beings; therefore, a careful study of the anatomy and physiology of the woman should give us more insight and understanding of her uniqueness, purpose and spiritual make-up.

Remember, both the man and the woman were created in the image and likeness of God, and as such, they are equal. However, God designed and created them differently, so that they can be interdependent.

You only have to take a glance at a man and a woman to know they are physically different. Even men who cross-dress as women are easy to spot because their behaviour and mannerism give them up.

Men and women think, act and behave differently. Men and women see and perceive things differently. This is just the way God created them both to be!

- In his book, "Straight Talk to Men and their Wives", the renowned Christian clinical psychologist, Dr James Dobson, said that, *"The Female physiology is a finely tuned instrument, being more complex and vulnerable than the male counterpart."*

It is obvious that God designed, created and built up the woman with much attention to every intricate detail, everything in its rightful place and functioning according to purpose.

- A van and a sports car are both vehicles, yet they are designed to function differently. They both perform the basic functions of transportation; however, because of their different purposes, they have different designs and specifications.

The same applies to man and woman. The differences in build, make-up and design were a deliberate act on the part of their Maker (God), because of the difference in function and purpose.

SOME MAJOR ANATOMICAL AND PHYSIOLOGICAL DIFFERENCES BETWEEN MEN AND WOMEN

(Adapted from "Dr Dobson Answers Your Questions," by Dr James Dobson)

1. The cells in the bodies of men and women are different. The difference in the chromosome combination (XY for men and XX for women) is the basic

cause of development into maleness and femaleness.

2. Due to the difference in chromosome combination, women have greater constitutional vitality than men. This means that, generally, women outlive men by three to four years. "Vive la difference!"

3. The skeletal structure of women is different from men. Women, generally, have shorter heads, broader faces (that is meant to enhance beauty), shorter legs and longer trunks. Men tend to have the opposite.

4. Women have more hair on the head and lesser on the body than men. Again, this enhances beauty, as the bible says, the woman's hair is her covering and glory.

5. Women have slower metabolism, which is a contributory factor to the easiness with which we gain weight. Now we know why…!

6. There is an obvious and remarkable difference between man and woman in the sizes of various organs. Women have larger stomach, kidneys, liver, and appendix (a necessary requirement to carry another life within the womb); however, women have smaller lungs.

7. The thyroid gland is also larger and more active in women. This is associated with smooth skin in women, relatively hairless body and subcutaneous fat, which are important elements in the concept of personal beauty. The Thyroid gland also contributes to emotional instability in women, which causes them to laugh and cry more easily.

8. Women's blood contains more water and, therefore, fewer red blood cells than men's. Since red blood cells carry oxygen to the body, the reduction causes women to tire more easily and be prone to fainting.

9. In brute strength men are 50% above women. Yeah!

10. The female brain is wired differently from the male brain. The hypothalamus, which is located at the base of the brain, and is often called the 'seat of the emotions,' is apparently wired differently between men and women.

    The way it responds to a woman's experiences, eg. trauma, can cause changes in her menstrual cycle, hair loss, moods etc; it also prepares her body during pregnancy.

11. Men have penises and women have vaginas, wombs and breasts.

12. Women have several very important functions totally lacking in men, namely, menstruation, pregnancy and lactation. They also have different hormones from men. All these influence behaviour and feelings.

It is interesting to note, however, that the major differences between man and woman are associated with reproduction.

So, let's celebrate and enjoy the differences, because God created both men and women differently, for a purpose!

CHAPTER ELEVEN

MOTHER OF ALL LIVING: A POEM

The name resounds from the beginning of time
A name, birthed from the loins of pain
For on that fateful day, when man fell from grace
And God pronounced judgement, not to His gain,
Adam rose and called his wife 'Chavvah'
The MOTHER OF ALL LIVING

What did Adam hear that day,
To give his wife such a name?
Oh, the voice of hope was so clear
For God in mercy had declared
That through the seed of Woman
Redemption shall appear.
Hope was rekindled, as God ordained
That in childbearing, woman would save the day

Mother, every woman's desire
For ingrained in her, at the very core of her being,
The urge to reproduce, she must satisfy.
For God has created her to function as the earth,
To take seed and multiply
Bringing forth the fruit of her womb

Rachel cried, 'give me a child or I die',
Hannah knew no peace until she conceived
Sarah had given up hope,
For she considered her body dead
The Shulammite woman, Elizabeth, all received
The seed of the womb and hope was alive again
For they could bear that name once again - Mother

The miracle of birth
Is but a fusion of the divine and human.
For heaven unites with earth,
When a seed is taken by woman.
This is the wonder of motherhood,

That a woman would take seed, incubate it,
And birth the fruit of that seed –
Another human being!

MOTHER, such a multifaceted name
Nurturer, Nourisher, Nurse,
Life-giver, Sustainer, Protector
Strength, Grace, Solution
Mother, a song in the ear of every child,
The sweet song of the fruit of the womb
Mother, the essence of womanhood,
Worthy to be honoured and celebrated

MOTHER
A name the Church must also bear
For, indeed, She is a woman,
The Bride of Christ, Her bridegroom.
Not only must She bear the name
The Church must also possess the nature,
The very essence of the name.

MOTHER OF ALL LIVING…
Church, arise to Motherhood
Bride of Christ, let the cry be heard from you:
"Give me children or else I die"

Zion, know no peace till you conceive
Church, draw to your Bridegroom in intimacy
Bride of Christ, take the seed His Word
And nurture, nourish and reproduce.
Church, bear fruit for Jesus Christ…
Knowing that the hope of humanity and all creation
Lies with you arising to MOTHERHOOD

By Jennifer Abigail Lawson-Wallace©2007

CHAPTER TWELVE

DESIGNED FOR PURPOSE (PART 1)

A greater part of our ministry is focused on and devoted to raising labourers among women, for the Lord. Women who would share the love of Jesus Christ with their families, communities and nations, and disciple them to walk in righteousness.

To be able to effectively fulfil this task, I had to do an in-depth study of the woman. After several years of studying and gathering information, and reading various books and articles about woman's anatomy and physiology, I wrote my second book in 2008, and titled it, **"DESIGNED FOR PURPOSE - Woman, Fearfully And Wonderfully Made."**

You may download a free PDF copy of it from our website, via the following link: https://womenintune.org/free-resources/ (Scroll down to locate the book. After downloading it, you may save it on your device).

AN INTRICATE INTERNAL DESIGN

God created and designed the woman uniquely and intricately, in every sense of her being, to enable her to reproduce the human race. Thus, she was created with a unique reproductive system, to accomplish the dynamic and important task of taking seed, incubating, multiplying, carrying and birthing life.

Unlike its male counterpart, the female reproductive system is almost entirely hidden within the pelvis; an indication of the hidden strengths of woman.

INTERNAL ORGANS:

The female reproductive system consists of several internal organs, namely,

1. A unique wiring of the brain
2. Two Ovaries
3. Two Fallopian Tubes
4. A Uterus (Womb)
5. A Vagina

HORMONES

A woman's body produces several hormones to aid the process of reproduction; below are the three predominant ones.

1. Oestrogen
2. Progesterone
3. Oxytocin

EXTERNAL ORGANS

Two Breasts - God designed and created the woman with two breasts for nurturing and nourishing a new born baby.

Women's breasts come in all shapes and sizes but perform the same task of nourishing and nurturing. This is the beauty of God's creation in woman.

EXCLUSIVELY WOMAN

All these organs and hormones are found exclusively in women, and not in men; this further distinguishes the woman and endorses her uniqueness.

- **Question**: The Word of God teaches us that the visible reveals the invisible; therefore, if women are this awesome and unique in the natural, what are they like in the spirit?

Psalm 139:14 TPT

"I thank you, God, for making me so mysteriously complex! Everything you do is marvellously breath-taking. It simply amazes me to think about it! How thoroughly you know me, Lord!" AMEN!!!

SOLE ABILITY TO MULTIPLY

Genesis 1:28 NKJV

"Then God blessed them, and God said to them, "Be fruitful and multiply; fill the earth and subdue it..."

This was God's mandate to humanity; the man and woman were to multiply, in order to exercise dominion on the earth. The man had the seed of humanity in his loins but did not have what it takes to multiply.

However, the woman alone was created with the apparatus, capacity, ability and capability to multiply and reproduce; thus, there would be no multiplication without her. As said earlier, whatever a woman receives she multiplies.

If a wife receives love from her husband, she would multiply that love, nurture and cause it to grow. She would grow to love and cherish, honour and respect him, and protect him with her very life, if necessary. However, if a woman is given abuse or insults, she is going to receive, multiply and incubate just that, and who knows what she would bring forth!

Wake Me Up At 5.00am

A man and his wife were having problems in their relationship and not talking to each other. About a week later, the man realised that he would need his wife to wake him at 5:00am the next day, for an early morning business flight. Not wanting to be the first to break the silence, he wrote on a piece of paper, *"Please wake me at 5:00am,"* and left it where he knew she would find it.

The next morning, the man woke up, only to discover it was 9:00am and he had missed his flight. Furious, he was about "attack" his wife why for not waking him up, when he noticed a piece of paper by the bed. The paper simply said, *"It is 5:00am. Wake up."* You can trust a woman to come up with something like that!

God designed and created the woman to multiply what she receives. Give her a sperm, which is invisible to the human eye, and she will multiply and nurture it, and labour to bring forth another human being. Give her a vision, a prayer request, or a burden for a sick friend, a city or nation. Once she receives it as seed, she will take it into her spiritual womb, incubate and multiply it.

God is seeking to place in us the seeds of His Kingdom - righteousness, peace and joy in the Holy Spirit. What we can do in the natural, we can do in the Spirit. This is why God is calling on women to rise up, come out of complacency and mediocrity, and possess our nations for Jesus Christ.

- **For Further Reading:** *Isaiah 32:9-17*

ABILITY TO BIRTH LIFE

Job 38:8-9 NKJV

"Or who shut in the sea with doors, when it burst forth and issued from the womb…?"

WHAT? The sea burst forth and issued out of God's womb, when it was created? Yes, this is how the sovereign God described the creation of the sea to Job! It issued forth and was birthed from His womb!

This, again, affirms the unique way in which the woman was created in the image and likeness of God! She was given the ability and strength to bring forth life. Indeed, *"the miracle of birth is but a fusion of the divine and human!"*

Let's now discuss the woman's reproductive process. Women everywhere need to know this and be empowered to celebrate and not despise this great and awesome ability that distinguishes them!

CHAPTER THIRTEEN

DESIGNED FOR PURPOSE (PART 2)

One of the most intriguing things about the female body is the way it functions, when creating life; almost like clockwork or an orchestra, pre-rehearsed and tuned-up.

THE PROCESS OF REPRODUCTION

1. Ovulation

The process of reproduction begins with ovulation, when an egg is released, ready for fertilisation and implanting in the uterus. Fertilisation takes place when the woman receives and takes a seed (sperm) from a man.

When no egg is fertilized and planted, the uterus sheds its lining and that results in the menstrual flow (aka period).

2. Pregnancy

Pregnancy takes place when the egg becomes fertilized and is implanted in the uterus (womb). The fertilized egg begins to develop into a foetus, as cells multiply, move, and differentiate. The foetus is nurtured and incubated within the womb until labour.

During this time the woman's body goes through a complete transformation, without any effort from her:

a. The lining of the womb (uterus) thickens to create a perfect environment of warmth and protection for the foetus.

b. Her hormone levels change to prevent miscarriage and her brain chemistry also alters.

c. Placenta, a disk-like structure that adheres to the inner lining of the uterus is formed and is connected to the umbilical cord, which links the foetus to the mother. Oxygen and nourishment come from the mother's blood via the placenta.

d. The woman's nutrients are automatically directed to go to the foetus first and secondly to her. Blood is carried from the foetus to the placenta and from the placenta to the foetus via the umbilical veins and arteries in the umbilical cord.

e. Amniotic fluid and membrane in the womb cushion and protect the foetus against bumps and jolts to the mother's body.

f. Even her centre of gravity changes so that she can keep her balance. This enables her to carry multiple foetuses.

g. Her breasts begin to alter and prepare for lactation

h. During pregnancy, the woman's entire body shifts focus and effort to the task of developing the new life within her.

Psalm 139:14 Voice

"I will offer You my grateful heart, for I am Your unique creation, filled with wonder and awe. You have approached even the smallest details with excellence; Your works

> *are wonderful; I carry this knowledge deep within my soul."*

Both women and men ought to know, acknowledge, appreciate, and praise and thank God for the awesome way in which He has designed and created women!

3. Labour

The next stage in the reproductive process is labour, which is a very crucial and stressful, yet, awesome and rewarding part of the life-creating process

> **Isaiah 66:7-8 AMP**
> *"Before she (Zion) was in labour, she gave birth; Before her labour pain came, she gave birth to a boy. [8] "Who has heard of such a thing? Who has seen such things? Can a land be born in one day? Or can a nation be brought forth in a moment? As soon as Zion was in labour, she also brought forth her sons.""*

The mother is often tired and has not much control over her body. She waits in anticipation and anxiety for the process of labour to begin.

The period of labour is one of much pain and effort. The severity of the pain and effort is due to the size of the baby.

What is incredible about labour is that the foetus the mother is birthing is larger than the birth canal, the vagina. It is just remarkable how God designed and built the female body to perform this awesome God-given function.

- It is said that the pressure exerted on a woman's body during delivery would kill a man! The pressure is so great that a man's body could not physically hold it. The magnitude of God's grace to a woman during labour is immeasurable.

- Personally, I believe that delivering a baby is both a physical and spiritual experience, because as she approaches delivery, the mother' body alters almost supernaturally, enabling her to accomplish what is almost impossible under any other circumstance.

The pelvis begins to shift, open up and re-align itself for labour and delivery. The foetus turns and aligns itself upside down, with its head toward the cervix. The walls of the womb begin to contract (stimulated by the hormone oxytocin), which is an indication that it is time for the baby to be delivered.

The contractions cause the cervix to begin to widen and open, and the baby's head presses on the cervix, which begins to relax and further widen in readiness for the baby to come out. When the cervix is fully dilated, with every nerve, muscle, fibre, energy and willpower, the mother pushes the life in her womb out. There is a sense of great expectation, excitement and joy as a new life is given to the world again!

- This is the miracle of life, that a 7-pound (or more) baby can be pushed through a 10cm hole! This is the miracle of life that a woman's body can sustain the pressure and pain. Indeed, God has fearfully and wonderfully created women! Hallelujah!

The umbilical cord is cut, signifying the separation of the newly birthed life from the mother's womb. The final stage of the birth process involves the delivery of the placenta. It separates itself from the lining of the womb, and through further contractions of the womb, the woman's body expels it.

The minute the placenta is shed, one life-birthing cycle ends and the body begins to prepare itself, in readiness to commence another. The ovaries begin to release eggs again in anticipation of fertilization.

- The impact of this awesome experience is huge, and should give us more revelation about our awe-inspiring God. The power and awesomeness of our invisible God are truly manifested in this outstanding and stupendous achievement through women.

- Woman, you deserve a standing ovation! God has truly honoured and empowered you. Indeed, you are a unique and fearfully and wonderfully made creation of God! Hallelujah

4. Lactation And Nursing

Isaiah 66:11 NASBS

"That you may nurse and be satisfied with her comforting breasts, that you may suck and be delighted with her bountiful bosom."

The labour stage, that travails and births a new life, is not the conclusion of the life-giving process of the woman. Once the baby's born, the woman feeds and nourishes it at her breast.

Lactation, the production and releasing of breast milk, is a complicated process that begins during pregnancy. Increased levels of hormones cause the milk glands in the breasts to grow and get ready for making milk. After birth, the milk glands begin to produce milk.

When the new-born baby begins to suck the nipple, a nerve impulse travels from the breast to the brain and causes another chemical, oxytocin, to be released. This, then, causes the milk glands and milk ducts to contract and milk is released into the suckling baby's mouth.

BREAST MILK AND BREASTFEEDING

The milk produced by a woman's breast is one of a kind; all attempts by pharmaceutical companies to duplicate it have been only partially successful. Breast milk contains the exact proportions of fats, proteins, carbohydrates, vitamins, minerals, and water that the new-born baby requires. It also contains thousands of different antibodies to protect the baby from potential infections, which manufactured formula lack.

Breastfeeding creates and allow a special bond and closeness between mother and infant. The baby continues to draw from the mother and its life and survival are solely dependent on her. The picture of a lactating and nursing mother is a very intimate and alluring one.

The mother continues to nourish and nurture the life that has been created by and through her. A mother never ceases to be a mother till death. In this the woman truly reflects the nature of God as El-Shaddai – the many breasted One, who nourishes and satisfies His people.

Isaiah 49:15 TPT

"Yahweh responds, "But how could a loving mother forget her nursing child and not deeply love the one she bore? Even if there is a mother who forgets her child, I could never, no never, forget you."

All in all, the reproductive capacity and ability of the woman permeates and influences every area of her life. It results in a greater appreciation for stability, security and enduring human relationships among women.

Unfortunately, one of the greatest deceptions of the enemy is to portray women as weak, subordinate and subservient. How could women be weak, with such an awesome capacity and strength to multiply and create and nurture life?

- Actually, the power and strength of the woman is encapsulated in one word, "PUSH!" If women possess such glory in the natural, what are they like in the Spirit?

CHAPTER 14

SIMILARITIES WITH THE HOLY SPIRIT

One awesome thing about the uniqueness of women, that is worth mentioning, is her shared similarities with the Holy Spirit. God created Man in His own image as male and female. This means that both male and female reflect the total image and essence of God on earth, as demonstrated in a family. The earthly family represents God's heavenly one. Indeed, the Bible tells us, in Malachi 2:15, why God created man and woman and brought them together as one.

> *"But did He not make them one, having a remnant of the Spirit? And why one? He seeks godly offspring…"*

Man and woman created in the image of God are to reflect the Triune God by reproducing and creating family on earth. In the Trinity, there is God the Father, God the

Son and God the Holy Spirit. In a family, we have a Man (father), Woman (mother) and Children(sons). If humanity truly reflects God's image, then it is very obvious that the woman's (mother) role is representative of the Holy Spirit's within the Trinity.

HE IS A HELPER

> **John 14:16**
> *"And I will pray the Father, and He shall give you another Helper (Comforter), that He may be with you forever"*

Of the two genders, women share more similarities with the Holy Spirit than men. Jesus described Him as One summoned, called to one's side or aid. He is an Advocate, One who petitions and pleads another's cause before a judge. He is One who pleads another's cause with one, an intercessor, just as Christ is interceding for us before Father God. He is a Helper, Aide, Assistant

After Christ's ascension to the Father, the Holy Spirit took His place with the apostles and disciples, to lead them to a deeper knowledge of Jesus Christ. He was also to give them the strength needed to enable them to fulfil the Great Commission, and undergo trials and persecutions on behalf of the divine Kingdom. The Holy Spirit will continue to do that with us, if only we will allow Him.

CHARACTERISTICS OF THE HOLY SPIRIT THAT WOMEN POSSESS

1. The Holy Spirit brooded over the earth at Creation. Mothers brood over their young. *(Genesis 1:1,2).*

2. The Holy Spirit is a Helper/Comforter. This is what God said of woman, when He created her. *(John 14:16; 15:26).*

3. The Holy Spirit is an Intercessor and prays for and through us. It is a known fact that more women take up and engage in intercession than men. *(Romans 8:26).*

4. The Holy Spirit is a Teacher. Statistically, there are more female teachers than men. *(John 14:26).*

5. The Holy Spirit pours out love. Even God asked, "Can a woman's tender love and care cease?" *(Romans 5:5; Isaiah 49:15).*

6. The Holy Spirit births us into the Kingdom. To become children of God, we are birthed by the Holy Spirit. Well, women give birth. *(John 3:5-8).*

The Holy Spirit is a dynamic force. If women are like Him, then women are not weak and ineffective as usually portrayed. Women have a dynamic, comprehensive, powerful and awesome nature, similar to the Holy Spirit.

CHAPTER FIFTEEN

SPIRITUAL LESSONS FROM A PHYSICAL REALITY

1 Corinthians 15:46 NLT

"What comes first is the natural body, then the spiritual body comes later."

The Word of God teaches us that the visible reveals the invisible, and that the physical precedes the spiritual.

The nation of Israel was first physical, and then following the death, resurrection and ascension of Jesus Christ, became spiritual.

Moses' physical tabernacle was a representation of the spiritual heavenly one.

The book of Colossians describes Jesus as the image of the invisible God, and Jesus Himself said that if you have seen Him, you have seen the Father. Therefore, we can learn about the spiritual by studying or observing the physical.

Romans 1:20 AMP

"For ever since the creation of the world His invisible attributes, His eternal power and divine nature, have been clearly seen, being understood through His workmanship [all His creation, the wonderful things that He has made], so that they [who fail to believe and trust in Him] are without excuse and without defense."

Psalm 19:1 NKJV

'The heavens declare the glory of God; and the firmament shows His handiwork."

The physical woman also has a spiritual glory. The woman was fearfully and wonderfully made in the image and likeness of God, therefore, by studying her physical body and her reproductive capacity and process, we are bound to discover hidden spiritual parallel truths.

SEVEN IMPORTANT LESSONS

There are several important spiritual lessons that we can learn about the woman. Knowing these should empower women and give them the confidence to offer themselves more freely and willingly to serve the Lord.

1. COMPLETE, FULL AND NEW IN CHRIST

It is without doubt that woman was created in God's image; therefore, her physical body reflects aspects of the divine nature.

Unfortunately, sin marred the nature of God in humanity; however, through Jesus Christ men and women are restored again. The fullness of God dwells in Christ, and men and women are complete in Him.

Both men and women have been made whole in Christ, and therefore, they can attain and achieve all that God has purposed for us.

> **2 Corinthians 5:16-17 TPT**
> *"So then, from now on, we have a new perspective that refuses to evaluate people merely by their outward appearances. For that's how we once viewed the Anointed One, but no longer do we see him with limited human insight. [17] Now, if anyone is enfolded*

> *into Christ, he has become an entirely new creation. All that is related to the old order has vanished. Behold, everything is fresh and new."*

It is important, therefore, to reiterate and emphasise, that women have been made whole, complete and new in Christ. Women can no longer be judged by the curse. Women have been made whole, complete and new in Christ and can exhibit those spiritual qualities that display the image of God in us. AMEN!!!

2. DESIGNED TO RECEIVE

Physically, God designed the woman to receive; this is an awesome part of her reproductive capacity. Spiritually, a woman's perception, intuition and discernment help her to receive. She is quick to perceive and within her spirit she can 'catch' and 'sense' things that are not very obvious to others. In the physical, also, she is uniquely designed to receive a sperm (male seed), and this also reflects her nature in the spirit.

A woman would receive or take anything - love or hatred, a business idea, a prayer need, a burden for a sick friend, a news report or a prayer request. Instantly, what she receives becomes a seed in her, with a full potential to germinate and bear fruit. It does not matter what it is, so long as a woman receives it, it becomes seed.

- All a woman needs is a seed. It is an unfortunate fact that these days, women can conceive and have children without intimacy with a man, just by acquiring a test tube of sperm. However, this proves the point that the woman all a woman needs is a seed.

Mary, the mother of Jesus received a word from the Angel Gabriel that she would conceive and bear a child, and she instantly received the word and took the seed of the Holy Spirit.

This is something husbands must remember, that a woman was designed to receive and whatever she receives becomes a seed in her being. Perhaps, that is why the scripture instructs men to love their wives.

When a woman receives love, it becomes a seed of love in her, which she multiplies and brings forth fruits of love. What women can receive in the natural is a mere shadow of what they can receive and carry in the spirit.

Another amazing thing about the woman is that she is not limited to one seed. She has the ability to receive and take more than one seed at a time, incubate them in her womb and birth them. Naturally, women can carry twins, triplets, etc, demonstrating their ability to receive and carry multiple seeds.

Hence, a woman can take on more than one project, idea or prayer request and ministry. She can certainly receive and take the seeds of the Kingdom.

> Psalm 68:11 AMP
>
> *"The Lord gives the word [of power]; the women who bear and publish [the news] are a great host."*

3. SHE MULTIPLIES WHAT SHE RECEIVES

As she is in the natural, so is she in the spirit, therefore, whatever a woman receives she multiplies. A woman receives a male seed and instantly her body begins to multiply, incubate, nurture and cause it to grow.

In the same way, if a woman is given abuse or insults by her husband, she is going to receive, multiply and incubate just that, and bring forth disrespect, anger, spite and even, hatred.

- However, if a wife is loved by her husband, she would receive and multiply that love, nurture and cause it to grow. She would grow to love and cherish him more and more. She would honour and respect him, and protect him with her very life, if necessary. Interestingly, because of the way God created men, the wife's expressions of love, would cause her husband to shower more love on her, which she would further receive and multiply. This cycle of love is the foundation of a good marriage.

Women always multiply what they receive. Like a snowball effect, whatever you give to a woman will multiply in her heart and hands. Give her a vision, a business idea or dream. Once she receives it, she will multiply it, (often on her knees, in prayer).

Jesus Knew This Truth!

Jesus knew this truth, and so when He was ready to reveal Himself as the Messiah and His mission on the earth, He went all the way to Samaria, to meet an unnamed woman at a well. (John 4). Upon receiving the Good News that Jesus was the promised Messiah, the woman immediately left her waterpot, and went and spread the news in her city. Samaria experienced revival as a result of her actions.

John 4:39 NKJV

"And many of the Samaritans of that city believed in Him because of the word of the woman who testified..."'

Once again, when Jesus rose from the dead, the first people to hear and spread the news of His resurrection were women. Yes, Jesus first gave the seed of the Gospel to women; they were the first to receive and share it.

John 20:17-18 NKJV

"[17] Jesus said to her, "Do not cling to Me, for I have not yet ascended to My Father; but

> *go to My brethren and say to them, 'I am ascending to My Father and your Father, and to My God and your God.'" [18] Mary Magdalene came and told the disciples that she had seen the Lord, and that He had spoken these things to her."*

God is seeking and raising women, who will receive the seed of His word, the Good News of His kingdom, and multiply it in their families, communities, societies and nations. May women (and men) everywhere be encouraged and empowered to also rise up and serve the Lord Jesus.

4. SHE BIRTHS WHAT SHE HAS MULTIPLIED

In the natural, whatever a woman receives she multiplies, and whatever she multiplies, she labours to birth. We see this ability manifested spiritually, especially, in the area of prayer and intercession.

It is a known fact that more women attend prayer meetings, and there are more women intercessors, than men. A woman can take an idea or a prayer topic to heart and will pray and work through it till it manifests.

The American preacher, Bishop George Searight, said, *"When I have a seed, an idea or problem, I give it to my wife. She goes down on her knee and labours until she births the answer."*

Without Her You Will Have No Ministry

A Pastor dreamt that he had died and gone to heaven, and God was giving out rewards. He realized that most of the people around him were his congregation members, which made him very glad. The Lord began to hand out crowns, calling each person by name. There were crowns of different styles, shapes and sizes; and some had more gems and precious stones than others.

Suddenly, God brought out the most beautiful crown that the pastor had ever seen. This crown had very large precious stones, which sparkled in the light, reflecting the colours of the rainbow. The pastor thought, "Surely, this must be my crown!" After all, he had worked so hard and led many to the Lord, and most of his congregation were there with him in heaven.

But no, God called out a quiet old lady in his church and placed the crown on her head. The pastor was perplexed, and asked God why. God said to him, "Without her you would have no ministry, because everything you have achieved is because of her prayers." God continued, "Every time you go up to preach, this woman goes into the cloakroom and prays for you."

The pastor woke up and realised it was only a dream. Yet, he was still perplexed by what he had heard in the dream and decided to verify it. The next Sunday, just before he was about to preach, he paused, walked through the puzzled congregation, and went to the cloakroom. Sure enough, he found the little old lady in the dream on her knees praying for him!

This dear old lady had taken her pastor and his ministry as seeds in her spiritual womb, and travailed and laboured for him on her knees for years! The fruits in his life and ministry had been birthed through her prayers!

- The bible says that "Deep calls to deep," and when a woman takes seed into both her physical and spiritual wombs, she becomes directly connected with the 'womb' of God. She is instantly linked with the ultimate Life-Giver and something profound takes place; a strong partnership is formed, as together, new life, solutions and answers are birthed.

The four Gospels give many examples of women who received, multiplied and laboured for the Lord: the woman at the well, the gentile woman who wanted her daughter healed (she would even settle for crumbs as long as she received something from Jesus), and Mary, the mother of Jesus.

Luke 8:1-3 mentions some more women in the bible… *Mary Magdalene, Joanna, Susanna, and many others.* Every one of these women had received a healing touch or deliverance from Jesus.

They sacrificed all and followed Him, providing for Him from their substance. They were utterly devoted to Him and served Him with their all.

Strength To Push!

There are further lessons to be learnt from a

woman's ability to labour and birth. The reason why a woman goes through so much pain and travail during childbirth is that what she is releasing and birthing from her womb is much, much bigger that the channel through which she is releasing it.

The determination with which she pushes and forces the baby out of her, goes beyond the natural. This ability can be channelled into the areas of prayer, intercession, evangelism, and in fact, anything we set ourselves to do.

- Perhaps, the vision or burden God has given you seems huge and impossible. Perhaps, the responsibility your pastor has placed on you appears too big. Perhaps the burden for your community nation is too heavy. Praise God for that, because as you link up with the Holy Spirit, He will supply grace and enable you to do what God has put on your heart to do.

C. Peter Wagner wrote that certain spiritual gifts are gender biased, including intercession. He said he interviewed several intercessors who suggested that a woman's biological function of conception, gestation and the travail of giving birth might have something to do with it.

A major purpose of the ministry of intercession is to bring forth the purposes of God; thus, intercessors often describe some of their most intense periods of intercession as travail.

Women know even better than Apostle Paul, the full meaning of his statement, *"My little children, for whom I labour in birth again until Christ is formed in you"* (Galatians 4:19).

5. SHE HAS STRENGTH TO ENDURE

Another parallel truth about the woman is her strength to endure.

Pregnancy takes approximately nine months. It is an extended period of waiting, anticipating and enduring patiently (or sometimes, impatiently). The ability to wait and endure, knowing there is not much one can do until it is time for the baby to come out is one of the strengths of the woman.

She endures the nausea and sickness, weight gain/loss, backache, bizarre cravings, mood swings, swollen ankles and clothes that don't fit.

Yet, she is focused and has her eye on the goal - a new-born baby boy or girl. She knows that 'though it tarries it shall surely come', so she endures and perseveres and presses on towards her day of delivery.

This is a great asset the Church needs, as we face a world full of evil and woe; warring for our marriages, families, communities, cities and nations.

Sometimes it is a real struggle to make change, as the things that work against us almost seem unmoveable and unshakeable. But with God, nothing shall be impossible!

Bringing Transformation

Societal and national transformation does not happen overnight. It takes time, effort and labour to birth righteousness in a nation. If there is nothing else that women can do, at least they can unite and persevere in prayer. We can contend for our communities, and not give up until we see the desire changes begin to manifest.

Isaiah 66:7-8 TPT

"[7] Zion gave birth suddenly, even before going into labor. She delivered a son without any painful contractions. [8] Who has ever seen or heard of such a wonder? Could a country be born in a day? Can a nation be birthed so suddenly? Yet no sooner does Zion go into labor than she gives birth to sons!"

Yes, it will not be easy. Yes, it takes time and effort, but, that is why God is calling on women! Their inherent strength of endurance; their ability to endure nine long months of pregnancy, accompanied by heartburns, backache and swollen feet. These unique characteristics and qualities enable women to press on, focused and undeterred until change comes. We can certainly go the long haul and endure the length of time it takes to bring change in our families, communities and nations!

The truth is that, unless we rise up, and we take these burdens, unless we carry, travail and labour over our families, communities and national, we shall not see the changes that we desire, and things will deteriorate further. With the help of the Holy Spirit we can birth the fruits of righteousness and peace in our lands. AMEN!!!

6. SHE NURTURES THE CHILD SHE BEARS

A woman's nurturing ability goes beyond the carrying and delivery of her child; she breastfeeds or bottle feeds the child till the time of weaning.

She continues to take care of that life she has birthed into this world, almost all her life. Hannah weaned Samuel and released him to the Lord in the care of Eli. Yet every year she made and took him new clothes.

A mother would sacrifice all for the welfare of her child. A mother would go to the ends of the earth to defend or protect her child. This is a natural ability that portrays the very nature of God as our Provider, Defender and Protector.

She Is A Discipler

There is an urgent need for disciplers in the kingdom. Newly converted souls must be discipled, raised and nurtured to maturity.

When I got saved many years ago, someone was assigned to disciple me. I attended discipleship classes, prayer meetings, etc, where I was nurtured and taught the basics of the Christian faith.

There were times when I felt like giving up, but the people around me supported and nurtured me, teaching me how to pray, fast, study and live the scriptures and share the gospel. I became grounded in the Lord as a result of this.

Unfortunately, there appears to be a shortage of people who would take time and effort to disciple others. There are many Christians who have not acquired a solid foundation and are struggling with sin, temptation and personal weaknesses because they were not properly nurtured and discipled as young Christians.

This is where, I believe, women could be of great benefit to the Church. Women are 'disciplers.' We have the natural ability to raise and disciple children. We can channel that ability into nurturing, nourishing and raising spiritual children for God. I know most women lead busy lives, but I believe if we cared enough, we would ask God for the strength and grace to do it.

Raising The Next Generation

> **2 Timothy 1:5 NLT**
>
> *"I remember your genuine faith, for you share the faith that first filled your grandmother Lois and your mother, Eunice. And I know that same faith continues strong in you."*

Timothy's faith had been passed on to him from his grandmother Lois, through his mother Eunice. This is trans-generational discipleship! Lois had nurtured and raised her daughter, Eunice, in the knowledge and fear of God; together, the two of them raised Timothy, who became the first Bishop of Ephesus.

Naomi raised Ruth. Elizabeth mentored Mary. Women can be a great asset in discipling and raising the next generation for the Lord. Amen.

7. SHE IS MULTIFACETED IN NATURE AND ABILITY

The final spiritual lesson that we can learn about the woman is her multifaceted nature and ability. Years ago, my son came into the kitchen and asked what I was doing. I replied that I was cooking the evening's dinner and two other dishes for the weekend.

He seemed very surprised and asked, "How are you able to cook three dishes at the same time?" I laughed, because what he did not realise was that I was also doing the laundry and dishes, and working on my computer at the same time!

- That is what you call multifaceted, multitalented and multitasked! And that too is a gift from the Lord to women!

Women with young children, especially those who have twins or triplets, manifest skills that surpass those of a company executive, juggling their duties - changing nappies, bathing, feeding, burping, putting to sleep, washing clothes, sterilizing bottles, doing the school run, and still having time to cook and clean! Wow!

Naturally women are able to multitask; which they also reflect spiritually!

Jesus Gives Us Strength

I Timothy 1:12 NLT

"I thank Christ Jesus our Lord, who has given me strength to do his work. He considered me trustworthy and appointed me to serve him."

Someone once asked me, *"How do you do it Jennifer?"* This is because I am devoted to Jesus Christ, and I am also a wife, mother and homemaker, run a ministry in several countries, mentor several leaders, am an author, graphic designer, publisher, and travel often to speak… and still make prayer and the word a priority in my life!

I answered, *"God gives me grace and strength!"* Like the woman in Proverbs 31, God has made me a multifaceted human being, and as I tune-in and rely on Him each day, I am indeed able to do all the things that He has committed into my hands. It is not easy, but the Lord supplies grace and strength, for each day and each task.

Philippians 4:13 NLT

"For I can do everything through Christ, who gives me strength."

THE CHURCH NEEDS THE GRACE OF GOD ON WOMEN

The Church needs the grace of God on women; we need the spiritual gifts and abilities of women, more than it has been acknowledged. Therefore, we need to ask the Father to show us how women can use their multifaceted characteristics, abilities and capabilities to benefit His kingdom.

Women can give life to anything that is dead. What is dead or dying in your church or community? What needs life? What needs nurturing? What can be influenced for the Kingdom? Just name it and place it in the hands of women; they will take it and transform and breathe life into it.

Matthew 9:37-38 NLT

"[37] He said to his disciples, "The harvest is great, but the workers are few. [38] So pray to the Lord who is in charge of the harvest; ask him to send more workers into his fields.""

The Lord needs labourers to preach the Gospel to all community, society and nation. He needs workers to raise disciples for His Kingdom. Women can handle that, if they are encouraged and properly trained and released to do that.

May the Lord Jesus Christ give women the grace to surrender and release themselves to Him, to be used for the glory of His Kingdom. AMEN!

CHAPTER SIXTEEN

THE CHURCH: THE ULTIMATE WOMAN

The greatest spiritual impact of these physical lessons about the woman, however, must be on the Church, the Bride of Jesus Christ. As the Bride of Christ, the Church is the ultimate woman, in the Spirit; therefore, she must possess the same spiritual characteristics, uniqueness and glory of the woman.

Let Me Explain...

> **Genesis 3:15 AMP**
> *"And I will put enmity (open hostility) between you and the woman, and between your seed (offspring) and her Seed; He shall [fatally] bruise your head, and you shall [only] bruise His heel."*

After the Fall of Man, God declared that the hope of overcoming sin, restoring life, and fulfilling His plans and purposes on the earth no longer lay in the hands the first Adam, but rather, another coming Adam, the seed of woman, the last Adam, who is Jesus Christ

> **1 Corinthians 15:44-45 NKJV**
> *It is sown a natural body, it is raised a spiritual body. There is a natural body, and there is a spiritual body. [45] And so it is written, "The first man Adam became a living being." The last Adam became a life-giving spirit.*

The first Adam was a living being, that is, soil into which God put His image and living Spirit to become an animated human being. The bible, however, describes the last Adam as a life-giving spirit, that is, the actual image and Spirit of God, which was put in the first Adam to make him a living being.

Now, it was not good for the first Adam to be alone. The task of reproducing after the image of God could not be accomplished because the essential female qualities needed were missing. In the same manner, the Last Adam needs His own Bride to accomplish the task of multiplying and filling the earth with the glory of God.

God created the woman to be a wife, help-meet comparable for the first Adam; a counterpart – also a living soul, created in God's image, of the same kind and nature, and befitting. Likewise, God is creating a Bride, a counterpart, of the same kind and befitting to the Last Adam. He is a life-giving spirit; therefore, His Bride must also be a life-giving spirit.

From that moment, onward, the destiny of humanity shifted from the first Adam to the last Adam, Jesus Christ, and His Bride, the Church. *(Revelation 12)*

BEE FRUITFUL AND MULTIPLY

Matthew 28:18-20 NKJV

And Jesus came and spoke to them, saying, "All authority has been given to Me in heaven and on earth. [19] Go therefore and make disciples of all the nations, baptizing them in the name of the Father and of the Son and of the Holy Spirit, [20] teaching them to observe all things that I have commanded you; and lo, I am with you always, even to the end of the age." Amen.

The task of populating the Kingdom and taking dominion on the earth has been given to the Church. Jesus commands us to be fruitful and multiply, and the Holy Spirit was sent to help us do just that! Through Him, God is preparing and enabling the Church to fulfil her purpose on the earth.

When women rise up and take on the responsibility of the Great Commission, the Church becomes more productive, and more souls are birthed into the Kingdom.

Again, in his book "Why Not Women," the late Jamie Cunningham, founder of YWAM, said that he would rather have one woman with him on the mission field than fifteen men; because he would need fifteen men to help him accomplish the task of one woman, on the mission field.

It is time for women to realise what we have and our value to the Kingdom. We do not have to wait for anyone to tell us what to do. We are part of the Church, and as we yield ourselves to Jesus Christ, the Holy Spirit will enable and empower us to build the Church and extend her influence on the earth, together with the men.

CHAPTER SEVENTEEN

DISCOVERING IDENTITY AND PURPOSE

Before I conclude this book, it is necessary to mention that all humanity is searching for significance and purpose. The fall of humanity displaced both the man and the woman from their secure place and position in God, leading to a loss of identity, significance and worth. *(Genesis 3)*. Mankind (both men and women) continues to seek these in diverse ways, e.g. name, fame, wealth, position, power and status; outside of a relationship with God.

However, for women, the search for identity, purpose, significance and worth, has been even more challenging.

This search traversed the centuries and appeared to have peaked with the Feminist Movement, which won many equality victories for women, i.e., the right to vote, right to education, equal opportunities in employment, etc.

Unfortunately, it also failed women by insisting that men and women are the same, and that women assert themselves by behaving like men.

(We have already determined in this book that men and women are equal, but different and interdependent).

Also, unfortunately, feminism's victories are still not enjoyed by women in many parts of the world, and so the woman's search for identity, significance and purpose continues.

DILEMMA

Women now face diverse dilemmas. For example, the modern educated woman soon realises that despite her various successes and achievements, etc, she is still unfulfilled; she still has other battles to fight against the ignorance, prejudices and biases of her culture, about the woman's identity and purpose.

The woman who lives in a village somewhere in Africa, Asia or South America is bound by culture and tradition's negative and demeaning portrayal of women.

The Christian woman struggles to see and define herself in the light of the Gospel that saved her, as the Church insists on defining women in Christ differently from men in Christ, and setting limitations for them.

The search for identity, purpose and significance, unfortunately, continues.

GOD-DISCOVERY, NOT SELF-DISCOVERY

However, as Christian women, our search for identity and purpose must not be one of self-discovery, where we are trying to find out more about ourselves, but rather, of God-discovery. This is because in order to find out who we are, and discover our true nature, characteristics and identity as women, we must discover God and His nature in the woman.

The woman was created in the image of God, therefore, AS HE IS, SO ARE WE. God's attributes are manifested in the physical, and His nature is entwined with every aspect of our being.

This is why I have given an in-depth description of the uniqueness of the physical identity and make-up of woman; to give us more insight into the nature of God in women, who are fearfully and wonderfully created in His image and likeness.

> ***Psalm 139:13-16 NLT***
> *"[13] You made all the delicate, inner parts of my body and knit me together in my mother's womb. [14] Thank you for making me so wonderfully complex! Your workmanship is marvellous-how well I know it. [15] You watched me as I was being formed in utter seclusion, as I was woven together in the dark of the womb. [16] You saw me before I was born. Every day of my life was recorded in your book. Every moment was laid out before a single day had passed."* AMEN!!!

IT JUST DOES NOT SERVE GOD'S PURPOSE!

We started this journey of discovering the uniqueness of woman, by asking you to picture a world without women. The intention was to encourage you to reflect and discover your worth as a woman, by examining what the world would be like if God had not created the woman.

I reiterate that many cultures and cultural practices and traditions degrade and relegate women; many consider women as subordinate and insignificant. Sadly, these views are also prevalent in the Church, and have caused many women not to truly discovered their full worth and position in Christ.

I reemphasise that this does not serve God's purpose, because, it has caused the Church (in many nations) to operate under-capacity by limiting and under-utilizing the gifts and callings of women! This has created a major setback to the fulfilment of the Great Commission, because in relegating women, the Church has inadvertently made more than half of God's workforce redundant.

The simple truth, therefore, is that just as a world without women would not serve God's purpose, a Church that that does not regard and empower women and give them their rightful place in Jesus Christ, would not fully serve God's purpose

UNIQUE

Again, the truth is that the woman is unique among all of God's creation. The man is also unique, but the sole focus of this book has been on the uniqueness of the woman; in order to help the Church to understand the urgent need to strengthen and empower women to serve the Lord.

A MEANS TO AN END

God is restoring and raising women to serve Him. It is, therefore, time to discover and celebrate the uniqueness and purpose of women. It is certainly time to celebrate their tender but awesome and powerful feminine characteristics, and acknowledge and truly appreciate their value.

However, the discovery and celebration of the uniqueness of women must not be an end in itself, but a means to an end. As women discover who they are in Christ Jesus and their purpose in God, they must rise up, empowered (by God, the Church and themselves) to fulfil that purpose.

Genesis 2:18 AMP

"Now the LORD God said, "It is not good (beneficial) for the man to be alone; I will make him a helper [one who balances him - a counterpart who is] suitable and complementary for him."

This is how the Church shall be victorious; because to discover the uniqueness of woman is to further discover the uniqueness of the Church, the Bride of Christ. As women discover and exhibit the nature of God in them, the Church will begin to manifest that very nature and fulfil her destiny and assignment as the Bride of Christ.

AMEN!!!

CHAPTER EIGHTEEN

THE FATHER NEEDS YOUR WOMB

One of the greatest phenomena in the bible is when God sent an angel to a young teenage woman to ask if He could borrow her womb. Actually, He did not even ask, but informed her that she had been chosen to take and carry the Seed of the Messiah in her womb, and bring forth Jesus, the Saviour and Light of the world.

Mary's response. upon hearing the words of the angel, would continue to resound throughout the ages:

> *"Behold the maidservant of the Lord! Let it be to me according to your word."*

Today, like Mary, the Sovereign God has chosen us, and is giving us an opportunity to carry and birth the fruit of Christ's Kingdom, that is, Righteousness, Peace and

Joy – in our communities, towns, cities, nations and on earth. *(Romans 14:17)*

UNDERSTANDING WHAT IS AT STAKE

However, the Father wants to give us an understanding, and a broader picture of what is happening and what is at stake. To do that, we must, again, return to an incident that took place in the Garden of Eden; to the serpent's judgement, which holds an important clue and key to the redemption of humanity and restoration of all things:

> **Genesis 3:15 NASBS**
> *"And I will put enmity between you and the woman, and between your seed and her seed; He shall bruise you on the head, and you shall bruise him on the heel."*

In judgement, God, Elohim, declared that there would be a blood feud between the serpent and the woman; there would be perpetual enmity and hostility between them. Secondly, there would be enmity between the seed of the woman and the seed of the serpent. He shall bruise the serpent on its head, and the serpent shall bruise Him on the heel.

- As discussed in Chapter 16, the woman, in the natural is you and I, and the female gender in general. In the spirit, however, the woman is the Church, the Bride of Christ. The seed of the woman is Jesus Christ, the seed of God, who was born both in the natural and by the Spirit.

The serpent's judgement was set in stone, by God. As the appointed time, Jesus Christ, the seed of woman prevailed over the enemy through the Cross and by His Resurrection; He conquered sin and death, and reconciled us to God by His Blood.

However, the enmity or blood feud between the woman and the serpent has continued through the ages till date. The bible has depicted this all the way from Genesis to Revelation. In Revelation 12, we see the woman with Child and the serpent (now a dragon) ready to kill that child.

- The plight of women throughout the ages has been a result of this judgement, as the enemy has sought to oppress, destroy and kill women.

However, one thing we have clearly seen throughout the bible and already discussed, is that whenever God's plan of bringing His Kingdom and will on earth was about to be destroyed or jeopardised, the LORD would often raise a woman to produce a seed, through whom He would fulfil His plans and purposes.

We have already discussed some of these women in Chapter Nine. However, it is worth mentioning that when the time came for the Messiah to be birthed, God further raised three women (including Mary) to facilitate His birth.

We have Ann (the widow who took the seed of prayer and intercession and laboured for decades for the Messiah to be born), and Elizabeth (the barren woman who, in her old age, took seed to birth John the Baptist, the forerunner of Jesus).

THE ONE COMMON FACTOR

The one thing that all these women had in common was the simple fact that they were women, created in the image of God with the ability and power to take seed, travail and reproduce. They used who they were in the natural, to fulfil God's spiritual plans and bring them into manifestation.

BIRTHING REVIVAL

Our world is in a predicament and in dire need of help; the only available solution is a spiritual awakening that would bring a fresh revelation of Jesus Christ and His Kingdom upon the earth.

We earnestly and urgently need the help of the Holy Spirit to proclaim and demonstrate God's Kingdom to a tired, sick and dying world! We need revival, a fresh outpouring of the Spirit, that would cause many to repent and enter the Kingdom!

God has promised a global revival; a move of the Holy Spirit that would sweep across the nations. Therefore, He is stirring up women to rise up, carry, birth and nurture this fresh outpouring of His Spirit.

> **Isaiah 32:11-12,15-17 ESV**
> *"[11] Tremble, you women who are at ease, shudder, you complacent ones; strip, and make yourselves bare, and tie sackcloth around your waist. [12] Beat your breasts for the pleasant fields, for the fruitful vine... [15] until the Spirit is poured upon us from on high, and the wilderness becomes a fruitful field, and the fruitful field is deemed a forest. [16] Then justice will dwell in the wilderness, and righteousness abide in the fruitful field. [17] And the effect of righteousness will be peace, and the result of righteousness, quietness and trust forever."*

Historically, women have always been actively involved in the revivals of the nations, and it seems the Lord is, yet again, calling on women to spearhead the prayer movement that will bring revival in these days! God is placing a burden and mantle of prayer and intercession for the nations upon His daughters.

- However, revival doesn't happen easily or by chance; revival must be CARRIED and BIRTHED.

Revival happens because someone takes it upon themselves to do something! Someone takes hold of heaven in prayer and prophetic intercession until heaven moves! Someone takes the pain to incubate and birth that revival through passionate prayer and intercession.

Revival does not happen overnight. It takes time, requires focus, and involves commitment, intense travail, persistence and perseverance.

ARISE MIGHTY WOMEN OF VALOUR!

Matthew 11:12 NKJV

"And from the days of John the Baptist until now the kingdom of heaven suffers violence, and the violent take it by force."

There is nothing as violent as childbearing. Therefore, as women, the Father is calling on us to rise up and take the seeds of the Kingdom of Jesus Christ - righteousness, peace and joy in the Holy Spirit - and multiply seed, incubate and birth the Kingdom in our homes, communities, churches, villages, towns, cities and nations.

WHAT CAN WE DO?

There are several things you could do, as a way forward.

1. Yield and surrender yourself to the Lord Jesus Christ. Ask the Holy Spirit to prepare and use you for God's glory

   2 Timothy 2:20-21 NLT

   In a wealthy home some utensils are made of gold and silver, and some are made of wood and clay. The expensive utensils are used for special occasions, and the cheap ones are for everyday use. [21] If you keep yourself pure, you will be a special utensil for honorable use. Your life will be clean, and you will be ready for the Master to use you for every good work.

2. Wait on the Lord and pray and ask God to show you what He wants you to do.

3. Spend more time in prayer, intercession and spiritual warfare. Engage in prayer walks and do prophetic acts, as directed by the Holy Spirit and word of God. You may consider forming a QUIVER prayer group. You may find out more about QUIVER at the end of this book or visit our website:

   www.quiverprayermovement.org.

4. Start sharing the gospel; take every opportunity to evangelize, lead others to Christ and disciple them when they come to the Lord.

5. Take responsibility for the political, economic and social climates of your cities and nation, and intercede for righteousness to prevail. Together, we can take responsibility for the political, economic and social climates of our cities and nations, and intercede for righteousness to prevail.

6. You may take responsibility for the next generation, praying for them, reaching out to them and instilling in then the fear

of God and the standard of His word. You may mentor and raise the next generation, and become a role model for them.

7. Give generously to fund the gospel, feed and clothe the poor, care for orphans and widows.

8. Above all, take the seed of the promise of God for revival and pray earnestly, labour and travail for a fresh move of the Holy Spirit upon the Church in the nations

Isaiah 32:9,11,15-18 NKJV

"[9] Rise up, you women who are at ease, hear my voice; you complacent daughters, give ear to my speech. [11] Tremble, you women who are at ease; be troubled, you complacent ones; strip yourselves, make yourselves bare, and gird sackcloth on your waists. [15] Until the Spirit is poured upon us from on high, and the wilderness becomes a fruitful field, and the fruitful field is counted as a forest. [16] Then justice will dwell in the wilderness, and righteousness remain in the fruitful field. [17] The work of righteousness will be peace, and

> *the effect of righteousness, quietness and assurance forever. [18] My people will dwell in a peaceful habitation, in secure dwellings, and in quiet resting places."*

God is colling on women to rise up! Our homes, communities and societies can be safe again, if only we rise up to build the kingdom! "Peace on earth and goodwill toward men" can become a reality in our homes, communities and nations, when we embrace the righteousness of God in Christ Jesus!

> **Isaiah 66:7-8 TPT**
> *"[7] Zion gave birth suddenly, even before going into labour. She delivered a son without any painful contractions. [8] Who has ever seen or heard of such a wonder? Could a country be born in a day? Can a nation be birthed so suddenly? Yet no sooner does Zion go into labour than she gives birth to sons!*

AMEN!!!

CHAPTER NINETEEN

ARISE AND SHINE

I travel the nations with a mandate from God to stir up His daughters, and raise, restore and release them to worship and serve Him. Many of the women I encounter are broken, wounded, afraid, helpless and weak. They have been abused and battered by life, and ensnared by culture and tradition.

Even though they have become God's children, many of the women I've met have no real sense or experience of God's love for them, or the value He places on their lives.

Many of them lack purpose and vision, and have no real perspective of a fruitful life in God's kingdom.

I am not referring solely to women in Africa, but also, women in the Western world. Whenever I think of these women my heart aches and breaks.

GOOD NEWS!

John 8:32 NKJV

"And you shall know the truth, and the truth shall make you free."

However, God has given me good news for every individual woman. YES, EVEN YOU!! God wants to put value on you once again. Through Jesus Christ, the Father is restoring you once again.

Psalm 45:13-15 NASB

"[13] The King's daughter is all glorious within; her clothing is interwoven with gold. [14] She will be brought to the King in colourful garments; the virgins, her companions who follow her, will be brought to You. [15] They will be brought with joy and rejoicing; They will enter into the King's palace."

Through this book on The Uniqueness of Woman, God has revealed deep truths about the woman. YES, ABOUT YOU!! You are fearfully and wonderfully made in God's image and likeness. His nature is within you. His strength and power are yours to possess. His favour is upon you. He loves you!

Therefore, it is time to arise and shine WOMAN, for God's light has come and His glory has risen upon you. It is time to take these truths and allow them to set you free, by changing your mindset.

May these truths about your uniqueness set you from EVERY yoke and bondage of culture, tradition and human limitations (even within the Church). ARISE, WOMAN! SHINE! In Jesus' name! HALLELUJAH!! AMEN!!!

Micah 4:13 ESV
Arise and thresh, O daughter of Zion, for I will make your horn iron, and I will make your hoofs bronze; you shall beat in pieces many peoples; and shall devote their gain to the LORD, their wealth to the Lord of the whole earth.

CHAPTER TWENTY

IT'S A NEW DAY: A POEM

The night dragged on and on,
The sun had long withdrawn.
Despair had begun its fight,
As the moon hid its light.
Paralysed by fear's grip
The mind awaited the dawn.

The seconds ticked by,
Turning into minutes that lie.
Time seemed to stand still,
As darkness reigned free.
Hope yielded to a long sigh,
Dreams and desire lost their will.

Yet, as the darkness grew thicker,
And hope and faith weaker,
A gong sounded loud and clear.
The voice of the herald heard,
Declaring for all ears to hear,
"It's a New Day!"

The dawn of the New Day is here.

The darkness flees in haste,
As the majestic sun rises fair.
The Sun of Righteousness arises,
Heralding the awaited genesis
Of a glorious New Day!

Fear trembles and despair fades,
As hope awakens and faith arises.
For not only did the herald declare,
A jewel so precious is made,
The sign of the New Day,
The pledge of God's care.

It's a perfect gift from God,
A sign of His faithfulness.
Another opportunity to live,
And His goodness to receive.
A new song swells from within,
As joy declares, "It's a New Day."

By Jennifer Abigail Lawson-Wallace©2015

ABOUT WOMEN IN TUNE

Women In Tune is a global army of women, faithfully worshipping and serving Jesus Christ.

Women In Tune is a sub-ministry of Cedars House Christian (International)

INTRODUCTION

For far too long, more than half of God's workforce has been redundant, and the Church has operated under-capacity by limiting women; hence, many gifts and talents have lain dormant or been under-utilized. This has been a major setback to God's kingdom, because whilst souls are perishing, the Church has been slow in rising to full operational potential, by releasing women to work.

However, there is a move of God taking place all over the world. Through the message of the love of Jesus Christ, women are being empowered to rise up and come out of their 'boxes' to worship and serve God! Culture and tradition can no longer hold them back. Fear, religion and prejudice cannot stop them!

Nothing, absolutely nothing, can stop them! They will be instruments in God's hands for the final harvest of souls into His Kingdom. They will form a global army, a network of prayerful, godly and kingdom-minded women, who will influence and change their families, communities, societies, and nations with the Gospel of Jesus Christ!

Our message is simple and clear – Jesus Christ is coming soon and ALL believers, irrespective of gender, race or age, must be strengthened, equipped, empowered and released to proclaim the Good News of Jesus Christ to all nations.

WOMEN IN TUNE was founded in 2002 by Apostle Jennifer Abigail Lawson-Wallace, together with her husband Rev. Cobby Emmanuel Wallace, by the leading of the Holy Spirit.

- **WIT is a non-denominational ministry dedicated to helping women grow to know and walk with the Lord and**

discover their true identity and purpose in Him.

OUR VISION

Psalm 68: 11,12

"God Almighty declares the word of the gospel with power, and the warring women of Zion deliver its message: "The conquering legions have themselves been conquered. Look at them flee!" Now Zion's women are left to gather the spoils." (TPT)

Our Vision is:

- A global army of women, faithfully worshiping and serving Jesus Christ.
- Women, who have been set free to love, worship and serve God. Women who are in tune with God and obey His voice.
- Prayerful, wise and Spirit-filled women, full of faith and strong in the Word of God. Women, who are continually being transformed to reflect the image and character of Christ.

- Women, who have risen from the place of fear, weakness, oppression and mediocrity to effectively impact and transform their homes, families, churches, communities, cities and nations.
- A global network of Kingdom-minded women, who are on fire for God and, together with men, proclaiming the Gospel of Jesus Christ.

Psalm 45:13-15

"The royal daughter is all glorious within the palace; her clothing is woven with gold. She shall be brought to the King in robes of many colours. With gladness and rejoicing… they shall enter the King's palace."

OUR MANDATE

Isaiah 61:1-4 NKJV

"[1] The Spirit of the Lord GOD is upon Me, Because the LORD has anointed Me To preach good tidings to the poor; He has sent Me to heal the broken-hearted, To proclaim liberty to the captives, And the opening of the prison to those

who are bound; [2] To proclaim the acceptable year of the LORD, And the day of vengeance of our God; To comfort all who mourn, [3] To console those who mourn in Zion, To give them beauty for ashes, The oil of joy for mourning, The garment of praise for the spirit of heaviness; That they may be called trees of righteousness, The planting of the LORD, that He may be glorified." [4] And they shall rebuild the old ruins, They shall raise up the former desolations, And they shall repair the ruined cities, The desolations of many generations.

OUR MISSION:

Ephesians 4:12-13

"12...To prepare God's people for works of service, so that the body of Christ may be built up until we all reach unity in the faith and in the knowledge of the Son of God and become mature, attaining to the whole measure of the fullness of Christ."

Our Mission Statement is:

A global army of women, faithfully worshipping and serving Jesus Christ.

Our Mission is:

- To raise women from a place of mediocrity to their rightful status in God.
- To raise Spirit-filled and God-fearing women of prayer and the word; women of strength and purpose, who would recognise God's voice and respond in obedience to it.
- To identify and expose the customs, traditions, beliefs, prejudices, and cultural and religious strongholds that have worked against and held women in bondage for so long, and to align these with the Word of God.
- To teach, train, equip and empower women to discover their place and fulfil their role in the family, Church, community, society and nation.
- To raise role models for the next generation of young Christian women and men.
- To raise intercessors and mobilise prayer

and intercession for the Church and nations.

- To go into the nations and raise 'labourers' to fulfil the Great Commission. *(Matthew 28:18-20)*

- To promote effective teamwork between men and women, in order to build, enhance and advance the Kingdom of God. Our aim is to strengthen the church by bringing women up to work alongside them. *(Genesis 2:18-23; Ephesians 4:11-16)*

- To preach the Gospel of the Kingdom and demonstrate the power of God in every nation we operate in, in preparation for the return of Jesus Christ.

OUR STRATEGY

2 Timothy 2:2

"And the things you have heard me say in the presence of many witnesses entrust to reliable people who will also be qualified to teach others."

- WOMEN IN TUNE offices/branches in all nations
- Regular meetings, conferences, seminars and workshops, etc.
- Teaching and discipleship programmes, including the FREE TO SERVE and DISCOVERING IDENTITY AND PURPOSE Discipleship Programmes.
- Empowering, raising and releasing the next generation of women to serve the Lord, through Women In Tune Youth.
- Youth Outreaches and Trainings
- Publications and literature – books, booklets, magazines, newsletters, blogs, articles, etc.
- Leadership mentoring programmes for women, young women and girls (teenagers and adolescents).
- Prayer meetings, retreats and prayer training, to raise and intercessors for the Church and mobilise prayer for nations.
- QUIVER Prayer Groups - mobilise women to form prayer groups of five to

pray for their nations.

- Economic empowerment: education, vocational trainings, sponsorships, etc, for women to gain employable skills, support for small businesses, etc.

- Evangelistic Outreaches and missions.

- Multimedia - social media, a website, online teaching resources, TV programmes, including, Let The Truth Be Told Channel on YouTube, and Podcast, etc

- Liaise with Churches, ministries and other organisations.

- A network to offer support and accountability, and promote strong, effective and dynamic relationships among women in ministry.

"And they shall rebuild the old ruins, they shall raise up the former desolations, and they shall repair the ruined cities, the desolations of many generations" – **Isaiah 61:4**

WOMEN IN TUNE YOUTH

Women In Tune Youth (WITY) is the youth ministry of Women In Tune (WIT), a ministry dedicated to raising, restoring and releasing women to worship and serve Jesus Christ.

WITY is committed to raising a new generation of women who know their identity in Christ and who will be bold, courageous and zealous to serve Him by influencing and impacting the world around them, and fulfilling the mandate in Isaiah 61:1-4.

WHAT WE DO

- Building a community of like-minded young Christian women, by discipling and raising young women of faith – women full of the Holy Spirit, prayerful and in tune with God's word.

- We help young women to re-discover and restore their true identity and purpose as women in Christ.

- We encourage young women to discover and nurture their unique gifts and talents and use them to impact their generation.

- We raise and mobilise young women to pray for their families, communities, cities and nations.

- We are raising an 'army' of young Christian women, who through the power of the Holy Spirit, would go on and bring transformation and reformation wherever they are.

- Ultimately, our goal is to empower young women to reach out to the lost with the Good News of Jesus Christ, fulfilling the mandate of the Great Commission (Matthew 28:18-20)

CONTACT DETAILS

Please contact us for more information about WOMEN IN TUNE OR WITY, get on our mailing list to receive our daily devotionals or regular newsletter, or to request Apostle Jennifer Abigail Lawson-Wallace as a Speaker.

Email: info@womenintune.org

WIT Website: www.womenintune.org

WITY Website: wity.womenintune.org

Website: www.cedarshouse.org

Facebook: @womenintune

Instagram: @womenintune

ABOUT QUIVER PRAYER MOVEMENT

Every revival in the history of the Church has taken place because God took hold of men and women, who in turn took hold of God in prayer, until He poured out His Spirit afresh from on high and changed the hearts and lives of men. The various revivals worldwide have all been preceded by God moving the hearts of people to prayer.

Historically, women have always been actively involved in the revivals of the nations, and it seems the Lord is, yet again, calling upon women to spearhead the prayer movement that will bring revival in these days! What exciting times we are in, indeed! God is placing a burden and mantle of prayer and intercession for the nations upon His daughters. God is raising, rallying and uniting women (and men) to prayer.

QUIVER is simply small groups of 'ordinary' women (and men) praying for revival in their respective nations. Each group or 'quiver' consists of up to FIVE women, focused and fervently and ardently praying to God for revival in the nation. These prayerful women will become 'arrows' in God's hands to fulfil His purposes in their land.

QUIVER was originally started to mobilise women in the United Kingdom to prayer, but is now growing in many nations. The clarion call is out... WOMEN AWAKE, ARISE, PRAY AND FIGHT FOR YOUR NATIONS!!!

WHO CAN JOIN

Any and all Christian women from all Christian denominations are welcome on board.

- You do not have to be a leader to get involved.
- You do not have to be a seasoned intercessor to get involved, as we will offer the training and support that you need.
- Men may also form or join a QUIVER prayer group.
- All that is needed is the desire, decision and commitment to pray.

CONTACT DETAILS:

For more information about QUIVER or how to start or join a QUIVER prayer group:

Email: info@quiverprayermovement.org

Website: www.quiverprayermovement.org